DeathStar/rico_-chet

DeathStar/rico -chet

Judith Goldman

O BOOKS • 2006

This book is dedicated to those on all sides imprisoned, wounded, and/or killed
in the course of 9/11, America's war on terrorism, its war on Afghanistan, and its sec-
ond Iraq war.

Grateful acknowledgment to the editors of fora where this work has appeared: *fascicle;
Ghosting Atoms; Mirage; New Messes; P-Queue; Viz.: Inter-Arts Magazine; War and Peace; War
and Peace 2.*

n/cntnt

A nation that demands from its government nothing but the maintenance of order is already a slave in the bottom of its heart.

ALEXIS DE TOQUEVILLE, *Democracy in America* (1835)

The war on terror is not a figure of speech.

PRESIDENT GEORGE W. BUSH, remarks on Operation Iraqi Freedom and Operation Enduring Freedom (March 19, 2004)

In the photographs, people are watching something we can't see what's just beyond our shoulders has transfixed them. So.

We are fixtures for composition.

LAURA ELRICK, "Dream Helmet" (July 22–October 7, 2001)

OSI RIP(?) c.2/19/02–c.2/26/02

US plans to set up office of Strategic Influence (Pentagon Sets Up Office to Influence Public Opinion Overseas (Pentagon eyes propaganda campaign, disinformation to influence opinion on war (Pentagon office considers planting false news items (Media watchdogs troubled by possible Pentagon propaganda campaign (DOD vows new 'influence' office won't lie (Pentagon mulls planting false news stories (Pentagon Plan to Influence Opinion (Pentagon office set up to sway public opinion overseas (Pentagon would try to sway opinion in hostile, friendly nations (Pentagon would try to sway opinion in hostile, friendly nations (Bill Arkin discusses Pentagon's Office of Strategic Influence and use of propaganda (Office of Strategic Influence; Good Idea? (Telephone Psychics; Legitimate? Can Marriage Reduce Poverty? Should Governments Use Propaganda To Help War Effort? (Defense Department set up a new agency after September 11th to funnel information favorable to US to foreign journalists (Defense Secretary Donald Rumsfeld addresses new Pentagon agency (Rumsfeld Says Pentagon Won't Plant False Stories In The Press (Pentagon considers using disinformation: New office to mold opinion in war on terror (Propaganda (Iran: Radio says US government censoring war news to cover war crimes (War of the words (Lies, damned lies and Pentagon briefings (Managing the News (What US newspapers are saying (Pentagon adds spin to war on terrorism (Controversy over US 'information warfare' (PEN-TAGON WEIGHING DISINFORMATION CAMPAIGN (Bush Plans To Turn White House's Wartime Communications Shop Into Permanent Operation (Pentagon plans propaganda campaign to sway public opinion (Pentagon's PR war against terrorism (Pentagon plans to launch misinformation campaign (Department of propaganda will spread disinformation (Pentagon might use deceit in war on terror ('Office of Disinformation' (US plans to set up office of strategic influence under attack (Pentagon chiefs condemned for launching propaganda war (Disinformation a poor tactic (Pentagon plans to sway opinion in other nations (REMARKS BY SECRETARY OF DEFENSE DONALD RUMSFELD TO TROOPS PROVIDING PROTECTION AT THE OLYMPICS LOCATION: SALT LAKE CITY, UTAH (Pentagon weighs disinformation campaign; official says won't include lying to public (FIGHT-ING TERROR / THE MILITARY CAMPAIGN PROPAGANDA; PROPOSAL TO MAKE UP NEWS DECRIED (Hub-linked PR firm off to war—Feds award Rendon propaganda contract

(Rumsfeld denies Pentagon planning to use Office of Strategic Influence to plant false information in news media (PENTAGON'S NEW BLACK PROPAGANDA UNIT (Pentagon 'ready to lie' to win War on Terror (Pentagon: Office Won't Spread Lies (Pentagon denies plan to spread falsehoods through media to promote US war goals (DEFENSE WILL NOT LIE TO PUBLIC, FEITH SAYS (Why must good guys plant lies? (Pentagon will not lie to the public, but may act to mislead enemy (Long history of American covert action, activity (Pentagon's anti-terror propaganda (Office of Strategic Mendacity (This is intelligence? (Pentagon to Use 'Tactical Deception'

in Information Warfare: Official (Pentagon plans to sow seeds of misinformation (Developments in the aftermath of Sept. 11 (Developments in Aftermath of Sept. 11 (AGAINST TERRORISM: US STARTS A NEW WAR, FOR WORLD'S HEARTS AND MINDS; PENTAGON PREPARES FOR COVERT CAMPAIGN TO WIN PUBLIC OPINION, ESPECIALLY IN ISLAMIC WORLD (Not ready for prime time (Planting misinformation is blatant propaganda (Defense Dept. Divided Over Propaganda Plan; Critics Fear 'Information Operations' Could Backfire, Hurt Pentagon's Credibility (Sound Off: Should Truth be a Casualty of the War on Terrorism? (What's Behind All the Face Time for the Administration on Television These Days? (Govt fuels 'propaganda wars' with false information (PENTAGON MULLS DISINFORMATION CAMPAIGN (Pentagon Draws Criticism For Reported Plans To Spread Disinformation (Pentagon would try to sway opinion in hostile, friendly nations (Pentagon weighs disinformation campaign; official says won't include lying to the public (Pentagon Tales: True or False? (Defense secretary must squash deadly proposal; Rumsfeld should put an end to the sick notion that the Pentagon should spread disinformation. (New Defense Office Won't Mislead, Officials Say (Rumsfeld Says Pentagon Won't Plant False Information (PENTAGON CLARIFIES PROPAGAN-DA PLAN; US OFFICIALS DEFER 'LIES' TO OUTSIDE GROUPS (Plan to tell media lies on terrorism (NO OFFICE OF MISINFORMATION (Russia president's aide mulls over Pentagon's PR plans (Pentagon plans a barrage of lies (Office of strategic mendacity (PENTAGON ABANDONS PLANS TO TELL LIES IN FOREIGN MEDIA (Pentagon clarifies to whom the lie's told (Lies from officials are still lies, no matter how they're spoken; A new Pentagon office won't deceive us after all, the Defense Department pledges (Yastrzhembsky unaware of Pentagon's planned strategic influence office (US undermining freedom of the press: media watchdog (Media watchdogs hit propaganda war (Pentagon Office of Strategic Influence Takes Shape (US DOD Rumsfeld addresses strategic influence criticism (Rumsfeld promises Pentagon will tell nothing but the truth (We're still wondering about the moon landing (New Agency Will Not Lie, Top Pentagon Officials Say (Pentagon denies plan to plant falsehoods: Rumsfeld says new military office may engage in 'strategic deception' (Rumsfeld Vows Not to Lie; Using false information to mislead foes is a different matter, Pentagon boss says; Rumsfeld Vows To Tell Truth to American Public (Formation of new Pentagon office might be perceived by media as ministry of propaganda (Military says it won't lie to public; But US will deceive enemies (Stick to the facts (NO DISINFORMATION, PLEASE; THE PENTAGON SHOULDN'T LIE TO 'FOREIGN' MEDIA (THE LIGHTER SIDE (Pentagon's overheated information warriors doused with cold water (RUMSFELD CLARIFIES DISINFORMATION POLICY; SAYS ONLY 'TACTICAL' BATTLE-FIELD DECEPTION WILL BE EMPLOYED (Let's sack pack of lies; clarity begins at home (The thoughtless shackled mind (Truth: best offense and defense (Pentagon denies plan to spread false data (LATEST FROM PENTAGON: HONESTY IS NOT THE BEST

POLICY (Secret office reveals where Pentagon lies (AND ANOTHER THING: (Bush inner circle has no just cause to hide the truth; Put a stop to Pentagon disinformation (Defining propaganda, illegal deception (Question and verify: Fighting propaganda (The Artifice of War (Missing the target: The Pentagon's clumsy diplomacy is creating a public relations nightmare for the US (Lies from America will abet lies about America (FEINSTEIN LETTER TO RUMSFELD (Pentagon is an awkward fit in news business (Pentagon Dealing With Ethics Of Info-Warfare (Shush, let's just win it (Pentagon uncaps its mighty pen (Pentagon scraps plans to spread black propaganda worldwide (Office of Strategic Influence disinformation campaign ill-conceived, abhorrent (Pentagon deceit can do more harm (A WAR ON INFORMATION (We don't need Pentagon to use press as a weapon (Global Eye—Global Lie (A magnet of lies on compass of truth: Is it any wonder people don't trust authorities when the Pentagon plans to sow lies in the foreign press? (Whispering out of both sides (Disinformation could be for you (No lies needed to tell America's story (Info warriors cooled off (Shining the Light (MINISTRY OF TRUTH (False News Demeans the Sender As Well (True lies from the Pentagon (PENTAGON'S DISINFORMATION WOULD HAVE HURT CREDIBILITY (Shaky start for Rumsfeld's propa-ganda machine (Real-life stories are becoming more humorous than those any comedian could make up (War is peace, freedom is slavery: Truth really is stranger than fiction (TV plan makes war on reality (The pollution of truth (Disinformation nonsense (Big Brother revisited (To Defeat Terror, Defend

Truth; In subtle ways, the Bush Administration may be toying with the dangerous game of outwitting its enemies with disinformation (Pentagon's PR Consultants Have History Of Running 'Black Ops' (Defense Department opens new office causing sharp criticism (NEW BATTLE REQUIRES A NEW PR GAME PLAN (EVERYONE, FROM PR PROS TO THE PRESIDENT, HAS TO LEARN THE REAL DEFINITION OF PUBLIC RELATIONS (Strategic Influence, Lesson 1 (Rumsfeld asks staff to review whether new information office should exist (Rumsfeld asks staff to review whether new information office should exist (Rumsfeld expresses doubts on new propaganda office (Rumsfeld Says He May Drop New Office Of Influence (Rumsfeld May Shut Down Office Of Strategic Influence (Rumsfeld May Kill Pentagon Propaganda Office (White House Angered at Plan For Pentagon Disinformation (DISINFORMATION PLAN HAS WHITE HOUSE AIDES LIVID (Bush in favor of scrapping Office of Strategic Influence (Bush Promises Truth From Pentagon (Fate of information office in question; Bush promises 'We'll tell the truth' (Would we lie to you?; Defense Department promises no 'strategic' fibbing to journalists (A quick end for a bad idea (Urgent: Pentagon to Close Controversial Office of Strategic Influence (Pentagon's Office of Strategic Influence to be closed (Rumsfeld: Pentagon to Close Office (US to close Office of Strategic Influence, Rumsfeld says (PENTAGON WEIGHS CLOSURE OF NEW OFFICE AMID CONCERNS ABOUT DISINFORMATION (Pentagon to close 'influence' office (STRATEGIC INFLUENCE OFFICE 'CLOSED DOWN,'

SAYS RUMSFELD (Defense Secretary Donald Rumsfeld shutting down Office of Strategic Influence (DOD to close 'influence' office (Bush Seals Fate of Office Of Influence In Pentagon (Rumsfeld: Pentagon Closing Office (Rumsfeld Shuts Strategic Influence Office (Rumsfeld confirms close of Office of Strategic Influence (BUSH ASSURES NATION 'WE'LL TELL THE TRUTH' (Plans to lie to the world have been canceled, and we really mean it (Afterthoughts (It's Right to Put Kibosh on Disinformation (Propaganda Ploys by US Military (RUMSFELD REINS IN INFORMATION WARRIORS; Defense secretary understands truth plays big role in American arsenal (Newspaper report may hurt Pentagon credibility, former official says (GOVERNMENTS EXPLOITING FEAR TO INCREASE SECRECY (Pentagon plan has potential; City can use tactics of Strategic Influence (Truth trumps propaganda (Developments Tied to Terror Attacks (Developments in the aftermath of Sept. 11 (Democracy arsenal running a little low (Creation of Office of Strategic Influence producing negative reaction (Information office will face probe by Pentagon, US says (Disorganized at Defense (SOME

FEAR PENTAGON PROPAGANDA PLAN (The Free Flow Of Obfuscation (OUR OPINION (An office of 'strategic influence' or just plain lies? (An office of 'Strategic influence,' or just plain lies? (Pentagon closes Office of Strategic Influence (Pentagon shelves new office for lying ('Misinformation' office shut down (Rumors close propaganda agency (PENTAGON CLOSES OFFICE THAT SOME FEARED AIMED TO MISLEAD JOURNALISTS; RUMSFELD BLAMES MEDIA (RUMSFELD CLOSES PENTAGON OFFICE AMID CONCERNS (Pentagon Closes Besieged Strategy Office; Defense: The agency stirred misinformation claims. Attempts to mislead the enemy in wartime will continue, officials say (Propaganda office may be eliminated (PENTAGON SHUTS STRATEGY OFFICE AMID DISPUTE (A 'Damaged' Information Office Is Declared Closed by Rumsfeld (Pentagon scraps new info office (PENTAGON CLOSES DOWN PROPAGANDA DEPARTMENT (Controversial US unit closed after "media manipulation" row (Rumsfeld shuts down office criticized for propaganda role (Rumsfeld says Pentagon closing heavily criticized Office of Strategic Influence (Rumsfeld Confirms Pentagon Scrapping Office Of Strategic Influence (NEW US PROPAGANDA OFFICE OUT OF BUSINESS (Pentagon closes office in charge of propaganda; Agency had been criticized over plan to spread disinformation as part of war on terror (Rumsfeld closes office set up for propaganda (Rumsfeld Kills Pentagon Propaganda Unit; News Reports Decried As Damaging, Inaccurate (Rumsfeld cannot tell a lie: Propaganda office to go (Rumsfeld disbands Office of Strategic Influence (Pentagon Decision To Close Its 'False Information' Office Applauded By President Of Council Of Public Relations Firms (Pentagon pulls plug on much-maligned office (Pentagon's Office of Strategic Influence to be closed (Pentagon Closing Criticized Office (Lesson for Rumsfeld But did he learn it? (OFFICE OF STRATEGIC INFLUENCE EXITS; RUMSFELD DENIES AGENCY HAD PLANNED CAMPAIGN OF DISINFORMATION (WAR REPORTING

GOES HOLLYWOOD: PENTAGON RESTRICTS JOURNALISTS WHILE PROMOTING FICTION-AS-REALITY (Disinformation a discredit to America (False news blackout (Pentagon's black propaganda war (Is it the truth, or is it a lie? (Is it the truth, or is it a lie? (Mission accomplished; Pentagon: Office that would have planted news, and possibly lies, in foreign press succumbs to criticism. (Lies eclipse underage-drinking issue (Truth is the first casualty of war, common sense the second (DECEPTION IS PART OF THE ART OF WAR, BUT SHHHHHH! (Short-lived office shut (BRIEFLY PUT: (Does government lie? (Let's not join the world's liars (Beware of Americans bearing news (PENTAGON PULLS THE PLUG (What will Become of the Pentagon's Strategic Influence Effort? (Orwell Office, Farewell (STOP PRESS! IT'S NOT TRUE (Who Wants to Know? (Credibility rescued; Defense Secretary Rumsfeld cancels plans for a propaganda office (Pentagon's idea of lying was 'breathtaking' in its stupidity (Pentagon's idea of lying was 'breathtaking' in its stupidity (Believe It Or Not (True or False?; The Pentagon says it's closing its Office of Strategic Influence. We hope it's not lying. (Trying to get the message across without the lies (Speaking of influencing opinion (Washington didn't need new office to stretch truth (Information warfare (A victory for truth and trust (Believe it or not (Believe it or not (Still Open To Winks And Nods (US telling truth—about not lying (Preparing for perpetual war (Truth: The Best Propaganda (GOOD RIDDANCE TO A BAD IDEA (TWO GOOD MOVES; US rejects proposals for coups and fibs (Improving our image (D.C. SPIN (REPAIR US IMAGE WITH TRUTH, NOT LIES (Truth, lies and silence (BE SILENT (CREDIBILITY IS AMMUNITION IN WARTIME (Keeping Track of Propaganda Can Be a Full-Time Government Job (Truth Dodges a Bullet (Office of Strategic Influence thankfully has been shut down (THE OFFICE OF MARITAL INFLUENCE (Official lying's high cost (Hollywood at war (Kazakh paper criticizes abandoned Pentagon black propaganda plans (Office of Strategic Influence was un-American ('POST' ON POINT IN REBUKE OF FEAR-BASED POLICIES (Disinformation? US Viewpoints Need Promotion In Islamic World (CASUALTY OF WAR ON TERRORISM: JOURNALISM (An office of 'strategic influence' or plain lies? (Is it the truth, or is it a lie? (Terror fight undercut by careless words (The Rendon Group's Customer List (ANOTHER FRONT IN THE WAR (Pool-water taffy—come 'n' get it! (Pentagon appears to be trustworthy (Military-press relationship hasn't changed that much (A TIME TO LIE?; PANEL DEBATES THE VALUE OF SECRECY IN WARTIME (PLAN TO MIS-LEAD FOREIGN PRESS WOULD HAVE CAUSED DAMAGE (Strategic Influence Office Closed (Disinformation Follies (Lies, Damned Lies, And Spin Doctors—In a world that condones outright deception, stay true to the truth (Unchecked aid (Pentagon Official Explains Bush Administration's Controversial 'Military Tribunal' Policy (Disclosure (The Short Distance Between Secrets and Lies (Hearts, Minds, and The War Against Terror (Disinformation Dustup Shrouded in Secrecy (Nigeria; Media Morality And Immoral Policies (Secrets of the Yo-Yo's (Secrets of the Yo-Yos Secrets of the Yo-Yo Brotherhood (All The Leaks On Iraq Plans: Is This Clever Or Confused? (

~~off white~~

         the next hour, dying, the
            fire blew and the engines
        roared in, putting on,   speeded

Again,the
 sun gone down

    grown in the shoes, which are full

  the sky changes
    in ways I did not think of

   notice
       and others remembered

           —Larry Eigner, "Anyhow."

Because we suffer we acknowledge we have erred.

           —Friedrich Hölderlin, *Antigone*

//Like many, Ritaccio has tried to
tragedy.// //Earlier Thursday, British
church service for British victims
strange position, trying to separate
I've received from the enormous tragedy,"
honors those lost in the World Trade
RESOURCE META INDEX. Keywords: September
stick to his routine since Tuesday's
Prime Minister Tony Blair attended a
of the tragedy.// //"I'm in a
what I've done and the attention
Franklin says.// //Annual parade
Center tragedy.// //911 NEWS
11th, 2001, September 11, 911, 9/11,

9-11, world trade center, towers, pentagon,
tragedy, attack, news// //It was about
reached`West 31st Street about the
the tattered flags salvaged from the
footage of the towers bursting into
that blanketed New York City in the
symbol of tragedy.// //Bright orange
early days of the tragedy: "NYPD,"
medical treatment, the word "Searched"
survivors.// //Other talks will focus on
political violence; how the media
disaster; how the nation remembers
essential roots in legend [but] tragedy
legend in dramatic form. For legend is,
tendentiousness.// //A tragedy within a
on Sept. 10 near the World Trade Center.//
and less depression among the elderly
Afghanistan has triggered World War II
fostered a drive for unity and cohesiveness
has made people slow down and be more
has strengthened family ties.// //America
Has United a Nation: How each of us chooses
of September 11, 2001 in our scrapbooks
decision.// //Invention is incompatible
legend is not motivated by the search for
with tendentious purpose expressed in
history of a nation.// //Our American
September 11, 2001 the United States
probably go down as the greatest single
// //*Can you still hear me?/Can you answer
we were saying, Father.*// //The horror of
the suddenness of the strike without
of the intent, the catastrophic results
nation// //Tragedy creates a cause-and-
what may happen at any time or place

america attacked, airplane, bomb,
8:50 a.m. on Sept. 11 when word
tragedy in lower Manhattan.// //Like
wreckage and the endlessly replayed
flames, the missing-person fliers
wake of Sept. 11 are an indelible
letters on the walls recall the
"Hot food," a cross signifying
on buildings scoured for
how the attacks were an example of
reported the first moments of the
tragedies.// //Tragedy has its
cannot be understood simply as
by its very nature, free of
tragedy; Man's wife was last seen
//"I think we'll see fewer suicides
this holiday season." The war in
flashbacks for some retirees. It has
among Americans, young and old. It
caring toward one another. Tragedy
Unites: Scrapbooking a Tragedy That
to remember the horrific events
will be an intensely personal
with tragedy. For the reshaping of
tragic situations, but is undertaken
terms of legend, the primordial
Tragedy September 11, 2001 On
of America experienced what will
tragic event in our nation's history.
clearly?/No. I have forgotten/what
people killed, injured, traumatized,
warning, the stark maliciousness
to the normal life of the entire
effect chain that clearly reveals
because that is the way the world

operates. Tragedy therefore arouses not
implications for our future normalcy as we
and seminal beyond any other single
don't know if anything surpasses
Lynch, 57, a history teacher at
mushroom cloud is conceivably world-
of the story, a chapter, but not
cloud portends a bigger tragedy
not ultimately rank with the combined
War or the Civil War or the World Wars,
but no single act rises to the impact of
with the fact that it was played out
nation, live!// //"We are a younger
improve the world," said Ana of her
few of her elders have witnessed.// //A
has offered free European excursions
Center victims to help them recuperate
//National Association of School
Helping Children Cope Tips for Parents
tragedy occurs, such as terrorist attacks
like many people, may be confused or
Model calm and control. Avoid
Reassure children that they are safe
important adults in their lives. 3.
are in charge.// //The offer came from
of Carinthia province, who has come
opposing foreign migration to Austria,
eastern Europe.// //www.childrensaid
home.html// //Explain that the
police, firefighters, doctors, and the
are hurt and are working to ensure
//"My kids came home from school
said.// //Subject: News Clip about why
chance to see another country's editorial
the US isn't thought well of all over the

only pity but also fear.// //and the
have known it make this event unique
happening in our history.// //"I
Hiroshima or Nagasaki," says Tom
Westminster High. "To me, the next
ending. The twin towers are a piece
the end chapter. The mushroom
than a terrorist attack."// //It may
events that led to our Revolutionary
or the consequences of those events,
this horror, particularly coupled
before the very eyes of the entire
generation and we can use this to
memories of a tragedy whose scope
controversial Austrian politician
to dependent children of World Trade
from the tragedy, officials said.//
Psychologists A National Tragedy:
and Teachers Whenever a national
or natural disasters, children,
frightened. All Adults Should: 1.
appearing anxious or frightened. 2.
and (if true) so are the other
Remind them that trustworthy people
Joerg Haider, the rightist governor
under fire at home and abroad for
particularly from southern and
society.org/cas/wtc-tragedy/
government, emergency workers,
military are helping people who
that no further tragedies occur.//
and were confused," Sicurelli-Wist
America is united. We rarely get a
about us, the USA. When you think
world, read this editorial from a

Romanian newspaper.// //"They couldn't
to give money to help the children in
we were bombing the country."// //An Ode
united? They don't resemble one another
couldn't understand the whole
Out of that confusion was born the
family touched by the tragedy. And
real caring.// //Still, the American
million people into a hand put on the
the house/to carry libations, hurt by
complex tragedies occur, people tend to
events into a single, stark image,
forever seared into the nation's
people were killed on Sept. 11 in the
attacks.// //It allows them to grasp
with global politics, bitter emotions
has thrown a big spotlight on us,"
of the Johannesburg World Trade Center.
Association and the Building &
committed people, equipment and whatever
the cleanup and rescue operation for the
repeated thousands of times daily in
one problem, however, with this article of
book focuses on the "first responders."//
hero, the tragic sacrifice, differs from
final sacrifice.// //"The United States
never had an attack that was so brazen, so
//a first sacrifice in the sense of
new aspects of the life of the nation
time, in the middle of these attacks,
brave people go into those buildings."//
does not measure up to the demands of the
the life of the, as yet unborn, national
firefighters not featured in the calendar
the heroic stature of firemen, especially

understand why they were being asked
Afghanistan while at the same time
to America. Why are Americans so
even if you paint them!// //"They
concept, and neither could I."
idea to help just one American
not just with money, but with
tragedy turned three hundred
heart.// //I came in haste out of
the hard stroke of hands.// //When
mentally boil down a whirlwind of
Weatherley says.// //It has been
consciousness that more than 5,000
World Trade Center terrorist
and file away a moment swirling
and high crimes.// //"This tragedy
said Neels C. P. Swart, chairman
// //The Building Trades Employers'
Construction Trades Council
else was necessary to assist in
tragedy.// //The statistic is
reference to the tragedy. There's
faith: It isn't true.// //Smith's
//In respect of its victim, the
any other kind, being a first and
has had great tragedies, but we've
murderous, so evil," said Smith.//
representative action, in which
become manifest// //"At the same
we had 403 such extraordinarily
//The action destroys him because it
individual will, but benefits only
community.// //Some relatives of
think its saucy pictures diminish
after the tragedy of Sept. 11.//

//*But if you still are without shame*
Biasano went to the police station
station and asked whether he could
across the way.// //*reverence at*
life,/our Lord the Sun, and do not
names, Biasano printed a quotation
"I pray that our heavenly father may
bereavement"// //*and do not show*
//One subway rider scrawled below
heavenly father, and I still think
you?"// //*such that neither land/nor*
welcome// //Another rider wrote
But another jotted, in smaller
Do you have to get into a religious
//Complaints of bias attacks in New York
year. Nationally, 2,110 attacks were
who look like Arabs.// //*before the face*
of day can welcome// //Infuriated
Republicans to pull a television ad//
allowing these claims, as we teeter on the
the fabric of our culture.// //*using*
Center and New York City's Ground
recriminations are potentially
over fairness after a mass tragedy, and
//against Ohio Democratic congressional
"disrespectful" and "a new low."//
fester. Why should the family of a bond
family of a kitchen worker, when they
//As spectators of the action in the
those who enact their parts and who
//"To use such a horrible tragedy in a
all those affected by the terrible
political actors they could take
partially know, thus imitating
place in politics," added Rep. Nita M.

before the face of men// //So
inside the Union Square subway
put the poster up on the wall just
least the flame that gives all
show unveiled// //Above the list of
from Abraham Lincoln that begins,
assuage the anguish of your
unveiled/to him the pollution//
that, "I don't believe in a
9/11 was a tragedy. Is that OK with
holy rain nor light of day can
under that: "Fine with me."
print still: "This is a memorial.
debate now? Have some respect."//
jumped fivefold, to 135, in the past
reported against Muslims or people
of men/reverence at least nor light
Democrats on Sunday called for Ohio
//Perhaps the greatest cost of
edge of decades of litigation, is to
images of the destroyed World Trade
Zero area in an ad// //The
endless. Open the door to litigation
no one will ever be satisfied.//
candidate Tim Ryan, calling it
//Bitterness has already begun to
trader receive $3 million, asks the
receive only a fraction of that?//
play they could see a whole denied
were bound to the particular.//
political way is disrespectful to
events of September 11th"// //But as
part in a whole they can only
the actors on stage.// //"and has no
Lowey D-N.Y., head of the Democratic

Congressional Campaign Committee.// //The harder we strive to satisfy
each person's claim to fairness, the greater will be the perceptions of
unfairness.// //Tragedy is an imitation of action. To understand a tragic
plot, we must recognize the events as a connected sequence corresponding to
some general or universal pattern.// //The horror which descended upon
New York, the United States and the World on September 11, 2001 was
first and foremost a personal tragedy in which the loss of human life
cannot be adequately measured.// //What about deserving victims elsewhere,
like the father who drowned last year while saving three children from the
flooded Mississippi?// //"The real tragedy is not the rubble on the ground but
the people that were lost," Sylla said. "Several thousand people died and
with them went lots of education, lots of training, lots of expertise. That
human capital damage will take a long time to repair."// //With the
attacks destroying America's largest office complex, and workers
nationwide watching the horror unfold from their own offices,// //Is his
family less deserving than that of someone who happened to work at the World
Trade Center?// //The structure of tragedy itself exemplifies justice.// //The
World Trade Center tragedy will prove the greatest challenge that
has yet confronted the US workers' compensation system.// //The New
York State Bar Association has established a toll-free number,
(877)-HELP-321, for victims of the September 11 terrorist attack on the
World Trade Center in lower Manhattan to call for assistance with law-
related questions.// //Horrible and catastrophic events such as occurred
on Sept. 11, 2001, were never contemplated in the legislative
crafting of our nation's social, remedial insurance paradigm.//
//It is not only that tragic figures reveal value by strenuously defying
their doom (some do and some do not), but that the very fact of their
passing recalls to us their inestimability.// //"We must
all do whatever we can to help those affected by the unspeakable
tragedy of September 11," said NYSBA President Steven C. Krane of
Proskauer Rose LLP.// //Amid grief, sadness and despair, the injured
workers and their dependents are being directed to file claims through this
traditional administrative system, which has been enhanced by a
complicated series of collateral and emergency entitlement programs.//
//On February 12, Steven Chin Leung arrived at a commercial mailbox

store in Manhattan to pick up his
the more unusual attempts to exploit
Leung tried to fake his own death
avoid a criminal prosecution.// //"As
more than 1,300 lawyers in the World
members, and their clients."// //New
they have made no similar arrests but
possible phony death claims and identity
Center tragedy.// //Prezant and colleagues
firefighters and five department
duty because of respiratory illness that
tragedy. A total of 250 were on leave
//State Attorney General Eliot Spitzer
that allegedly are cashing in on the
expense of the legitimate fund-raising
//In a major defeat for World Trade
Silverstein, a federal judge ruled
tragedy was a single occurrence under
//The plot of a tragedy, being the
present it as a unified whole; and its
arranged that if any one of them is
effect of wholeness will be seriously
drawn a direct connection between
tragedies, experts say.// //The
structures aflame, then tumbling,
Americans have never before seen in a
veterans of workplace tragedies were
of the devastation they experienced
where the World Trade Center once
television. But the raw trauma of 9/11
years, something akin to the Challenger
week at the end of September was to
the construction crews// //a lone
world, says historian David Kaiser.//
steel and concrete amid the ash from

mail. He was arrested. In one of
the tragedy of September 11th, Mr.
in the World Trade Center attack to
a bar association, we can help the
Trade Center, many of whom are our
York state insurance officials said
are investigating several cases of
thefts stemming from the World Trade
said that as of August 28th, 358
paramedics were on leave or light
appeared after the trade center
with stress-related problems.//
is investigating several charities
World Trade Center tragedy at the
efforts of the FDNY and the NYPD.//
Center leaseholder Larry
yesterday that the twin towers
the policies of the insurers.//
representation of an action, must
various incidents must be so
differently placed or taken away the
disrupted// //many people have
their own workplaces and the
mental montage of the super-
represents a brand of swift violence
single morning,// //But even these
shocked and saddened by the enormity
at the field of debris in Manhattan
stood.// //let alone on live
could be just a grim memory in 25
explosion—// //Their job for one
identify safety hazards confronting
tragedy that didn't reshape the
//that are slowly untangling tons of
the two 110-story towers// //Nelson

smiled and spoke calmly to her
with a public tragedy that has been a
neighboring buildings that were
collapse.// //for her and her husband.//
Aristotle, the protagonist will
downfall—// //Sometimes, she is
that play in her head of the gaping
Center.// //not because he is sinful or
not know enough. The role of the
its moral status but from the
Hence the *peripeteia* is really one or
in blindness, leading to results
were intended// //"Sometimes, I feel
of me," she said.// //And the
essential knowledge that was
Weller, healing comes from immersion
who are using drugs and alcohol to
after the national tragedy, are the
said Joseph Califano Jr., president of
the problem.// //Individuals who have
tragedy have yet to begin to deal with
//Tragedy, [Raymond] Williams claims,
some abstractable part of it which
sensibility more than the rest.// //In
speeches, they've raised more than $11,000
the crowds, it's a story that brings home
therapy.// //*Approach and deign to touch*
not fear./No man but I can bear my
helped them cope with the tragedy, and as
more normalcy in each day.// // Those who
tragedy feared that Western New York could
terrorist attacks.// //Developers also
offices in a new skyscraper at the same
another attack, there is a general
a scene where a tragedy occurred.// //*What*

classes while struggling to deal
private nightmare// //and the
destroyed or damaged by the towers'
//In the ideal tragedy, claims
mistakenly bring about his own
overwhelmed by the media pictures
hole in the side of the World Trade
morally weak, but because he does
hamartia in tragedy comes not from
inevitability of its consequences.
more self-destructive actions taken
diametrically opposed to those that
like that big gaping hole is inside
anagnorisis is the gaining of the
previously lacking.// //For Frances
in the tragedy.// //"The Americans
cope, or have relapsed from sobriety
forgotten victims of Sept. 11,"
a Columbia University group studying
been through such an incredible
all of its ramifications.//
is the whole of this action, not
happens to engage a morose modern
baskets passed around after the
for the victims of the attack. For
the tragedy. For the three men, it's
me/for all my wretchedness, and do
evil doom.// //Counseling has
time passes, each has found a little
weren't personally affected by the
be a possible target for future
could have problems filling the
site. In addition to fear of
reluctance to be associated with
terror whirls you backward from

the door? What foulness then, unless some
victims butchered at the hearth./There is
//HOMETOWN VOICES: Q: What do you think
former World Trade Center?// //Getting
buildings is similar to the difficulty the
passengers to travel again. People have to
measures have been taken and their country
another devastating terrorist attack.//
be rebuilt, but there has to be some sort
tragedy." Joseph Rojas, Visalia// //many
sense of a senseless tragedy, to see in
unbelievable on television. // //"What
rebuilt because we need to move on and
should not be rebuilt to be as tall as
such assurances are given, everyone's
goes on. The deadly fire in the MGM Hotel
California earthquakes in years past also
convinced that the possibility for
been minimized.// //"The site should be
in the park, there should be either a
shows the names of all those lost in
Ivanhoe// //Roland Kraft & Associates
memorial building and statues dedicated to
three main office towers, a 1,200-room
York Opera House.// //Fred Rogers,
Rogers' Neighborhood," is taping five
on PBS. Sitting in front of his old
Rogers talks to parents about the
there's Oklahoma City, Waco, Texas, the
there, too, not physically, perhaps, but
on television as tragedy and destruction
likely to be confused," Rogers says in
what an anniversary is, and if they
television, they might think it's
put down the phone and waited. As

horror in the mind?/What then? Only
a breath about it like an open grave//
should be done to the site of the
tenants to feel safe in super tall
airline industry now has getting
be convinced that proper security
is doing everything to prevent
//"I think that it should definitely
of memorial to remind us of the
have been drawn to the site to make
person what looked so unreal and
should happen is that it should be
live our lives. In my opinion, it
it was." Sarah Toth, Visalia.// //If
confidence strengthens, and life
in Las Vegas and the destructive
had people afraid until they were
tragedies like this to recur had
made into a memorial park. Somewhere
wall or floor path or something that
this tragedy." Danny Gonzalez,
developed concept plans for a
the Sept. 11 tragedy, along with
hotel, an amphitheater and the New
longtime, retired host of "Mister
public service messages for parents
"Mister Rogers'" kingdom set,
tragedy's anniversary.// //Then
World Trade Center. We've all been
through the images played repeatedly
struck them.// //"Young children are
the TV spot. "They don't understand
see the tragedy replayed on
happening at this moment."// //She
she followed the mounting

tragedy on television, her concern
not in order to provide mimesis of
rather, their characters are included for
covering the tragedy, some members of
themselves in direct danger.// //Photos
as it unfolds, head shots of firefighters,
together their lives in the aftermath.//
appropriately felt in painful and
interfere with that pleasure.// //
all this time, reading about the tragedy
news, it has an air of unreality," said
courageously is pleasurable to the
circumstances "conceal" the pleasure.//
Lane," Ms. Murray said, "too far for me to
the attack. We could see a pile of smoking
While the Murrays agreed that the barriers
of the destruction, they were glad they
plot are the goal of tragedy, and the
all.// //"It was very emotional for us,"
Murray added: "It was the right thing to
the tragedy."// //But tragedy is imitation,
complicated by painful attendant
felt without interference.// //To
felt as their hometown became the
the world, the Vancouver group plans to go
Zero when they arrive Thursday.// //"A
says. "It's an educational institution
historical framework." But the enormity
to blur those distinctions, the curators
Breckenridge firehouse, Presbyterian
community gatherings help participants
the aftermath of this tragedy."// //I
beg you,/if you have any care for
is enough// //Tragedy is a literary
by actors in which a central character

heightened to panic.// //So it is
character that the agents act;
the sake of their actions.// //In
the media community placed
include action shots of the tragedy
and images of people piecing
//In real life, pity and fear are
distressing circumstances, which
"Because I've been in Westchester
every day and watching it on the
Mrs. Cho.// //In principle, acting
courageous, but the unpleasant
//"We were at Broadway and Maiden
get a true sense of the horror of
rubble and a crane working on it."
made it hard to see the full extent
went.// //Thus, the events and the
goal is the most important thing of
Ms. Murray said, "very sad." Mr.
do. It helped us grasp the scope of
not real, so pity and fear are not
circumstances; the pleasure may be
feel something of what New Yorkers
epicenter of a tragedy that shook
directly from the airport to Ground
museum is not a memorial," Siegfried
that provides an interpretive
of the World Trade Center loss began
found.// //Speaking at the
minister Frances McWilliams said the
"look for a glimmer of meaning in
beg you—do not hunt this out—I
your own life./What I am suffering
composition written to be performed
called a tragic protagonist or hero

suffers some serious misfortune
therefore meaningless// //"People
their solidarity with New Yorkers,
identity as Americans," she said.// //but
misfortune is logically connected with the
elevators, or "people movers," in the new
museum—rise parallel with the monument,
the glass floors and understand the
commits again another version of the error
built in Riverside County depicts the
the memorial is "about our common humanity.
what happened."// //and this means that
of repetitions of the "same" error.// //So
attacks on Sept. 11 on her television set,
understand the tragedy. For the next
sculpted a 3-foot-tall Statue of Liberty
towers with an American flag signed by
her shoulders.// //Praimnath recounted
services at the Visalia First Church of
"It was a day I saw the twins separated
to the Twin Towers and the Statue of
tragedy to snap us back into reality."//
share our talents in a way that hopefully
course of this tragedy," said Brian
director.// //Shaheen has become
impact of the current political climate
the Bush White House sent senior adviser
Nov. 11 in an effort to enlist the
terrorism.// //www.poetry.com With profound
site is available for posting poetry about
39,217 poems have been posted so far.//
body in last year's attack on the World
odds just by surviving. Hers is an
tragedy.// //The story that William
"American Ground" is that of the cleanup

which is not accidental and
were longing for a way to express
our unity as a nation and our common
is significant in that the
hero's actions.// //As the glass
buildings—part of which will be a
visitors will be able to look out onto
immensity of the tragedy.// //A text
it denounces,// //The artwork to be
World Trade Center tragedy. Noble said
It is us under pressure, us reacting to
all texts are potentially endless series
as the Temecula woman watched the
she turned to what she knows best to
several months, Moroz designed and
holding up the World Trade Center's twin
Temecula firefighters draped over
his tale as a survivor during three
the Nazarene on Saturday and Sunday.
from the lady," he said in reference
Liberty. "Sometimes, it takes a
//"This is an opportunity for us to
will touch other people during the
Anderson, Fremont High School's band
increasingly concerned about the
on depictions of Arabs in film since
Karl Rove to Beverly Hills on
entertainment industry in the war on
sorrow, a special section of our
the tragic events of September 11th.
//Burned over more than 80% of her
Trade Center, Manning, 41, beat the
uplifting saga, triumph amid
Langewiesche sets out to tell in
operation at ground zero—the

"unbuilding," as he puts it, of the World
to stay alive was captured by her husband,
he sent to friends and family during the
messages that became the basis for a
Lauren." A new paperback edition (Bantam,
problem with the book is that Mr.
just that—a heroic engineering project
the heady recovery effort that it was
that killed 2,797 people and rocked the
been the subject of articles in *The New*
"The Oprah Winfrey Show" and with Katie
rehabilitation, Lauren was visited by Sen
book he has written is less comprehensive,
blooded than recent television documentaries
Jagger took notice. To demonstrate support
star sent a guitar to Greg, a brokerage
for a bar band called the Rolling Bones.//
Saturday that the rebuilt bell tower
in Albuquerque's historic Barelas
beams found in the ruins of the Sept.
is that Matthew Arnold guiltily leaves
the 1853 edition of his poems, as too
age of ideological anxiety and smoldering
listing the victims of the World Trade
tower.// //Metal Management Northeast, the
handling some of the trade center debris,
agreed it would be used as a memorial to
or altered. "When you see it, you know it
Steven Phillips, a vice president of the
"There's a desperate need for people to be
historian in Massachusetts and expert on
brings the tragedy home," said Mark
the New York State Museum.// //Birds
3,000 acres on Staten Island, have always
metals company has bought 500 tons of

Trade Center.// //Manning's struggle
Greg, 45, in e-mail advisories that
initial phase of her treatment—
bestselling book, "Love, Greg &
$11.95) updates the account.// //The
Langewiesche treats the story as
—forgetting in his celebration of
occasioned by a national tragedy
nation's consciousness.// //She has
York Times and appeared with Greg on
Couric on "Today." During
Hillary Rodham Clinton.// // The
less objective and far more cold-
about ground zero.// //Even Mick
for the couple, the Rolling Stones
firm executive who also plays bass
//Archbishop Michael Sheehan announced
for the Church of the Sacred Heart
neighborhood will display two 20-foot
11 terrorist devastation.// //So it
his tragedy *Empedocles on Etna* out of
desolate and enervating a work for an
popular rebellion.// //A memorial
Center tragedy will be a part of the
Newark scrap recycler that is
donated the beam after the museum
the Sept. 11 tragedy, and never sold
was a tortured piece of steel,"
mining museum, said Thursday.// //
connected," said Nick Carpasso, an art
public memorials. "And having an artifact
Schaming, director of exhibitions at
at Fresh Kills, a dump that covers
been a nuisance.// //A Georgia
steel from the World Trade Center—

and is melting it into "commemorative
pop. The enterprise has sparked outrage
company officials are heartless profiteers
//"Obviously we want to preserve the
take things off the site, especially
lost in tragedy," said Hallie Pickhardt,
result, "God's Army," is a 27-page,
World Trade Center attacks through a
up publication expenses (about $ 5,000),
dedicated to a scholarship fund for
the tragedy, said Belcourt.// //"We
tragedy as much as we can," NSync's
Piguet has created 200 limited-edition
children through NSync's foundation,
//Belcourt also made sure that part of
student in the school the lyrics to her
cooperative effort between staff and
heartfelt response to an otherwise
11, the routines for many American
their gates, Pakistani storeowners
flags in the front to show allegiance.
load, which will be shredded and
another recycler, who will process
used by manufacturers. Eventually,
worst tragedies will be reborn as
fender, copper for pipes in homes, or
// //"Audemars Piguet is the right partner
as a reminder of goodwill and harmony that
tragic as the attack on the World Trade
RIDGE, Tenn. Two 10-foot steel girders
will now reinforce the memory of the Sept.
fashioned from those beams was unveiled
some 750 miles from Ground Zero—as a
the struggle to honor it.// //DNA testing
felt fortunate his company could help

medallions" that go for $29.95 a
from victims' families, who say
cashing in on tragedy.//
evidence. We don't want the birds to
if it's belongings of a loved one
a USDA spokeswoman.// //And the
soft-cover book that recalls the
faith perspective. After squaring
all proceeds from sales will be
families who've been hit directly by
want to help kids affected by the
Justin Timberlake said. Audemars
watches that also will benefit needy
"Challenge for the Children."//
the project included teaching every
favorite patriotic songs. The
students has proven to be a most
unspeakable tragedy.// //Since Sept.
Muslims have changed. After opening
in Midwood, Brooklyn, place American
// //Dawson bid $250,000 for the
bundled before it is sent off to
the metals into a form that can be
the scrap from one of the country's
anonymous parts: a car alternator or
part of a new toaster or refrigerator.
for designing a watch that will last
can come even from an event as
Center," Timberlake said.// //OAK
pulled from the World Trade Center
11 terrorist attacks. A memorial
Wednesday at Oak Ridge High School—
testament both to the tragedy and to
alone takes two weeks. He said he
out in the time of a national

tragedy.// //Argentine scientists have
communities learn the truth about
has been chaplain to the New York
1990 and said the team members,
in the face of adversity, have
the tragedy in their hometown.//
in gathering information about
//The protagonist should be renowned and
can be from good to bad.// //This nation
death camps, raised this lamp of liberty
plot is most likely to generate pity and
aroused by unmerited misfortune, fear by
ourselves."// //We have no intention of
latest gang of fanatics trying to murder
discovering, as others before them, the
great democracy.// //The White House
to drive their supporters to the
towers, under a flag unfurled at the
lost, we have made a sacred promise, to
not relent until justice is done and our
prepares to mark the one-year anniversary
150 communities in 36 states will be
tragedy.// //What our enemies have begun,
tragedy just plunge us deeper into fear,
of invulnerability through military force?
program was "to remind us of what that
to America, and to keep our heads up and be
were shocked," Price said of Williams'
he was a wonderful man."// //I believe
matched this nation with this time. America
//*And they who read the dream meanings/and
under earth/dead men held a grudge still*
//We respect the faith of Islam, even as
that faith.// //In late August, police
had in his possession 20 homemade

gone on to Zimbabwe to help
massacre victims there.// //Weber
Yankees baseball team since
though trained to stay competitive
been emotionally "flat" since
//Bosnian experts have aided
the World Trade Center tragedy.//
prosperous, so his change of fortune
has defeated tyrants and liberated
to every captive land.// //Such a
fear in the audience, for "pity is
the misfortune of a man like
ignoring or appeasing history's
their way to power. They are
resolve of a great country and a
used the tragedy of 9/11 as a means
polls.// //In the ruins of two
Pentagon at the funerals of the
ourselves and to the world: We will
nation is secure.// //As the nation
of the Sept. 11 attacks, more than
hosting peace events to mark the
we will finish.// //Or will this
violence, and the senseless pursuit
// //Price said the purpose of the
tragedy meant to us and what it meant
ready for any kind of attacks." "We
death. "God had a reason for it, but
there is a reason that history has
strives to be tolerant and just.//
*spoke under guarantee of God/told how
/and smoldered at their murderers*//
we fight those whose actions defile
arrested a Florida podiatrist, who
bombs and two anti-armor rockets

(among other weapons) and a list of 50
was at First Assembly on Sunday to
surviving the now-infamous al-Queda
tragedy motivated him to spread the word
our will, but to defend ourselves and
//The airline supervisor said: "These men
they're from the FBI." I knew my rights and
them, but I also knew that some Arab-
detained.// //This joint resolution may be
of Military Force Against Iraq."//
war of aggression against and illegal
for example, in his commentary on *Hamlet*,
tragedy is not just an illustration of the
//the United States forged a coalition of
people in order to defend the national
righteous destruction of ranting villains
criminal law, but none for true art. But
personages may interest, exalt, and
contract guilt by becoming opposing
forces, which by some misfortune come
was able to deal with this tragedy—and
received so much aid and encouragement
Whereas United Nations Security Council
all means necessary to enforce United
//The people of America made us feel
much, much bigger than even our own
more important:// //Whereas Congress
the war on terrorism through the
requested by the president to take
international terrorists and terrorist
the United States of America.// //As Doug
article, there is a silver lining in the
vote: "136 House members voted against
to go to war whenever he wants."// //When
Sept. 11, it's important to remember that

Muslim places of worship.// //John
tell his harrowing story of
terrorist attacks and how the
of God.// //We fight, not to impose
extend the blessings of freedom.//
would like to talk to you, I think
I knew that I did not have to talk to
Americans who refused to talk had been
cited as the "Authorization for the Use
//Whereas in 1990 in response to Iraq's
occupation of Kuwait// //When he refers,
to the famous graph of desire, the
graph, but, rather, the graph itself.//
nations to liberate Kuwait and its
security of the United States.// //The
and criminals has indeed an interest for
the tragic destruction of highly moral
reconcile us to itself when they
champions of equally just ethical
into collision.// //New York City
overcome it—largely because it
from the rest of the country.// //
Resolution 678 authorizes the use of
Nations Security Council Resolution 660//
that we were part of something
city, something much greater and
has taken steps to pursue vigorously
provision of authorities and funding
necessary actions against
organizations// //We were a part of
Ireland notes in his TomPaine.com
tragedy of yesterday's congressional
giving George W. Bush a blank check
we think about the horrible events of
we were attacked because of our beliefs.

// //We were attacked because we fiercely
economic freedom while the terrorists
oppression.// //But Americans are also
things the Al Qaeda is attacking:
believe these entrepreneurs are
they're still doing it well.// //But a
//Excited by their high-powered, low-risk
cadre of Pentagon officials and
plans to attack a host of other
"harboring" terrorists, whether or not
worst terrorist tragedy.// //Living in
and determination that you don't even
is placed in jeopardy.// //*gods have
mine it is to wrench my will, and consent/
beat down my edged hate*// //We should see
reminder that freedom and democracy come at
//*Terror, the dream diviner of/this house,
wrath/from sleep, a cry in night's obscure
house*// //And we must never close our eyes
values we fight so hard to preserve.//
as an epic Star Wars saga stifles
//Rudolph J. Giuliani is the former
portion of the proceeds received from the
to the Twin Towers Fund.// //*For many
of honor, yet break justice.*// //As people
undeniably, well, a horror and a tragedy,
to mount retaliatory attacks, here are
here.// //Tragedy is an exemplary cultural
between human intention and human action is
// //"And it is equitable to pardon
to the law but to the legislator;//
it is increasingly clear that Cheney and
to validate their dangerous delusions of
the law but to the intention of the
itself, but to the moral purpose; not to

believe in religious, political and
fiercely believe in tyranny and
taking advantage of one of the
capitalism. And whether or not you
exploiting a national tragedy,
free people will always prevail.//
victory over the meager Taliban, a
congressional leaders is hatching
impoverished nations said to be
they have any connection to America's
freedom gives you a reserve of bravery
know you have until your way of life
*forced on my city/resisted fate/And
to their commands, right or wrong/to*
the World Trade Center site as a
a heavy price—the price of vigilance.//
*belled clear, shuddered the skin, blew
watches, /a voice of fear deep in the*
to those who seek to tear away at the
//The depiction of national tragedy
questioning and critical thinking.//
mayor of New York. His
sale of this article will be donated
among men are they who set high/the show
recoil in horror at what is
and as the US undoubtedly starts
a few brief reminders of how we got
site where the inexorable split
displayed with unusual scrupulousness.
human weaknesses, and to look, not
//On this anniversary of Sept. 11,
his protégés have used the tragedy
grandeur.// //not to the letter of
legislator; not to the action
the part but to the whole"// //The

22

so-called War on Terror was always just
unilateral use of military power to
//Cardinal Egan echoed calls for calm,
justice in this tragedy,"// //Nine days
11, 2001, the Department of Justice was
drastically expand its ability to
suspected of "domestic terrorism."//
are clean of this murder?/How? How? Yet
some fiend to guide you.// //"as
which hatred and desires for revenge must
human conflict is irreducible in the
to know if we as black folks feel more
after the Sept. 11 tragedy because now
the Arabs.// //"I am sure that we'll allow
united community to be abused or accused
of individuals."// //Then publicity is a
site of conflict, if only a conflict
action.// //*The black ruin that shoulders/*
brothers/strides at last where he shall win
eaten.// //"Today, in the midst of deep
that grief, tragedy and hatred are only
and love have no end."// // The Pakistani
massacres of Taliban soldiers. One involved
troops, many of them students from
army south of Kabul.// //"The Lord of life
mourn," said the prayer, signed by Bush
to this commuter town, 20 miles west
Alliance forces were advised by British and
Kabul.// //Youth as far away as Siberia
happened 9/11 is a real tragedy for all
But at the same time, back in the US, a
this attack could alter anyone's values
presidential elections had a bigger impact
by Mayor Walter Long, the president
praying that Almighty God...will watch

an expedient reason for the
achieve global dominance.//
noting: "I am sure that we will seek
after the terrible tragedy of Sept.
already circulating a proposal to
investigate and prosecute those
//What man shall testify/your hands
from his father's blood/might swarm
citizens of a nation under God in
never have a part."// //The animus of
realm of appearance.// //He wants
relieved and less under the gun
the pressure is off us and on
no group or groups in our diverse but
because of the outrageous misdeeds
site of recognition because it is a
between the registers of speech and
though the streaming blood of
requital/for the children who were
pain and sadness, we must remember
for a time. Goodness, remembrance,
press today reports two alliance
the wholesale slaughter of 1,700
Pakistan who'd joined the Taliban
holds all who die and all who
and faxed on White House stationery
of Manhattan.// //The Northern
American military units inside
were also moved, writing, "What
[of the] world, not just [the] US."
boy in Florida, Sergei, said "how
puzzles me," arguing that the last
on his life.// //In the prayer, read
asked the throng to "join me in
over our Nation and grant us

23

patience, resolve and wisdom in all that
antagonism proceed the right and wrong of
true ethical idea, purified and triumphant
reconciled in and with ourselves.// //How
more of a connection with the attacks of
country where they occurred?// //*The place
/will be a heavy curse on them./One needs
that.*// //"Sadness is the only word I can
sadness. The tragedy in itself, the loss
part to deal with, the incredible loss of
Brooklyn when the planes hit.//

//it may be asked whether tragedy
//it may be asked whether tragedy
//it may be asked whether tragedy
//it may be asked whether tragedy
//it may be asked whether tragedy

is to come."// //Out of this
each party. There appears also the
over onesidedness, and therefore
can youth in distant Siberia feel
9.11 than a boy living in the
*you lie in—if it suffer wrong—
no god to have the knowledge of*
use. Just an overwhelming sense of
of life...That's been the toughest
life," said Crooke, who was in
//Don't turn tragedy into war.//

is possible without recognition//
is possible without recognition//
is possible without recognition//
is possible without recognition//
is possible without recognition//

case senSitive

I am the combat. I am not one of the combatants; rather I am both combatants and
the combat itself.   HEGEL, *Lectures on the Philosophy of Religion*

THIRD CITIZEN   We have power in ourselves to do it, but it is a power that we
have no power to do.   SHAKESPEARE, *Coriolanus* 2.3.4–5

the brothers there it began to click with them and I
said so what sorry suckers it took all this to make
you come 'round and look at us and not
the object lesson
                     HEATHER FULLER, "Apostal Decision (Time Sensitive)"

IN MEDIAS RES

"...and/or juno broke/blood from a
                              stone
Came to see who in place
that he would not Help, etc.

"So now doubt you alas/?

 [—] call the meeting to ~~order~~

"To anyone in the actual/
                              world/
Oration, etc.

"In being trained to
follow

companions going/Down
beneath the hands
            of

—transitive—

"Shares in the conflict and/or peril alas of
                                    combat, etc.

—intransitive—

"And/or always catch/
                    attention before
"Taking place/placement/place/of all
                            other re/
                            semblances
/only
what that/that good/Artillery/

at the vanishing/point/alas

"Right of/right/
right/to self-defense obtains

"Most avid onlookers/
Oration, etc.

"Do you wish to bring back a man, who alas
                                    is mortal or

beat him under/(beneath)/w/hands/out of
the strong encounter/?

"It is, as *I* said, proof
no-wrong has been done

 "HereHere

"So power me, depending me, print could/
justification
and/or even if he masters his
                                        rage

—intransitive—

"Appointed as refuge, death/
as far as/possible, models/every/
thing,/etc.,/alas/alike

"His own part and/or not to interfere

            "But not-all/the rest of us
            shall approve you/!

"Pending alas/details alas

 [—] re-call the meeting to ~~order~~

artificer Presiding, artifist.
                        president

aside: Capitulate/yet he Wept
            tears of blood

Such is the privilege: to the ground in all his
arms
merely obeying gravity before alas
and/or submitting to its
~~order~~

"Ahem, etc.

[—] prepare the ~~order~~

"Ain't it the shit/'twas
purest light of heaven for whose/fair
love they
                fell

"Heart in my breast balanced between
                                        and/or
tampered w/alas
mixed.Media/alas

"Here Here

"SupPose," to give an example, "suppose
an uproar were/to be heard/?—transitive—

testifies against/?—transitive—

"Muscle In, etc., lapse
into pointlessness and/or at once lose
hearing into sight/?—intransitive—

"Pricking it for pity/virtue virtue by/virtue
of virtue virtue virtue, etc./

            regime change alas/
virtue virtue in detention/they nothing doubt!/

"Prevailing, etc.

"What is meet/be said/it must be/"meet"

"Meet him later; blood, *now*
—transitive—

            "Flat wall, flat/riposte
            debt in its parodic form
            they got/got, etc.
            should be/let off/alas

"blood/parody: mixed.Media!

"Cut it! Quit it!"

 [—] Unprepare the ~~order~~

"Shucks
, as I said,
            alas
as dim lights vanish/in the rays of the sun
you who undertook, so now
doubt do you/?, etc./?"

"Meaningful epithet
Oration, etc.,

"And/or like a simple child, he is caught

["he is, like, caught

"On the field/of sacred duty
—transitive—
                              ["*way* transitive

"It's academic
your dove's look and/or my fox's heart/a
thing of/blood alas
whose/motion
timed with/dying cries, etc.
as if/there is a natural affinity etc.
when it is not-supported/by its
                              context

"Where there's smoke/there's
                    "smoke"/statistically

"Need cash?/Why wait?

          "To the wronged party who subsequently/alas gains advantage
          Oration etc.

          "Your metaphor, etc.,/ distracted
                                        me
from the "metaphor," etc.
seems okay, seems fine/to its own sacrifice alas
for a moment at/fault alas/as to the "crusts
of bread" and/or "such"/
the actual sounds/I was just
                              wondering/
(actual "sounds")/when it is not-supported
by its context,/ "such" is the privilege?

"Know what/t-t-to/look for/?, the t-t-tip
of the t-t-t-ongue, go/figure
w/a plastic knife and/or a conflict of interest—t-t-t-ransitive—

 :Exordium:

[Combat Tracker Team. WELCOME COMBAT TRACKERS TO YOUR WEBSITE "SEEK ON"
"TRACK ON" "CARRY ON" THANK YOU COMBAT TRACKERS FOR YOUR HONORABLE
SERVICE.] [Combat Air Museum. For More Information Contact Combat Air Museum Phone:] [UXN
SPAM COMBAT provides online tools] [Employment Opportunities at Wilson Combat] [the two compa-
nies would come together to correct any underlying differences to forge one identical property, that being
the Scott Firefighter Combat Challenge.] [At Air Combat USA, you actually fly a light attack fighter air-
craft] [The Ultimate Resource for Combat Simulation and Strategy Gamers! If you love personal comput-
er-based combat simulation] [Combat-Online: SAS and special forces, combat survival, terrorism,
bodyguarding] [US ARMY VIETNAM COMBAT ART.] [Publications Arts of Combat and Chivalry.
Equestrian Rules, Regulations, and Policies]

    —intransitive—

    [—] prepare to Unprepared the ~~order~~

"A sore point/and/or provocative/Shucks, Ain't
                                        it
my foot here, etc., alas and/or you standing on
                                        it/
confirm but do inhabit and/or the prospect of, etc.

"Shares in the conflict and/or peril alas of
                                        combat

    —intransitive—

"They are "at it"/

"Their noise be/
                    our instruction

"Snatches my sense/tampered w/

"The end results being this, that and/or the/

          —"Is the case"/pending, etc./?—

          "It is, "as *I* said," as I said, "proof
          no-wrong has been/done

          ", as I said,/" "But not-all/the rest of us
          shall approve you/!

"Cut it! Quit it!"

 "HereHere

          "So, Casing:

"Casing, etc., circumstances, etc.

               ". . . and/or juno broke/blood from a
                                        stone
before submitting to its ~~order~~ alas
only felt as fetters/strange feathers these
                                        letters, etc.

          "Why you . . . !"

aside: ritually paddled/dogmatism/hazed/it
is only right and/or proper/home on his

                                                          shield alas/
doomed/by his/
                              destiny, etc., alas

 [—] re-call the meeting to ~~order~~

"Supposing truth is a woman, see, and/or
Are there not-grounds/?

                                             ["Do you wish to bring back/
                                             ["You Who, like, Undertook

"The distance from earth to heaven, etc.
telescope, juno broke/submitting to alas
                                                   necessary to

"Where this innate/of Force?
repose of blood, so power me
Ain't it/the shit/?

"If it is left standing at all/?

 "HereHere

       artifist.
                  president
       Oration, etc.

              : "Disagreeing about/agreeing/to disagreement, can
       we come to a disagreement/agreeing to/disagree and/or going
       ahead anyway/what is there to, like, argue/let them hate, etc., as/long
       as they fear are/either in my side and/or against/self-made and/or
       the real pig, by the squeal, etc.

: "I'll be the judge of that

: "For there are scoffers who/claim that my fluttering pulse is the
squeal of what my sons and/or the sons of Pandu did with your swiss
army knife, etc., and/or a conflict of interest/having been very inexpert
alas having been duct-taped and/or slammed against
—transitive—
the fire escape

 "HereHere

: "Light of my life, fire of my loins

["light of my, like, life
["fire of my, like, loins

"Cut it! Quit it!"

: "Paler than the grass of the absolute of Force, "suppose," as I said,
"truth has been held down while his teammates/insert/my sin, my soul, the
seven-mouthed Nile/

—transitive—

The prospect of your dove's look
                              ["and/or my, like, mechanical precision

 [—] give the ~~order~~

"Give it!

"Give it t-t-t-o me!!!

"Shucks, Ain't it/the
                    shit/?

—intransitive—

   "But in the first/case/alas

"In case/?

      "In case/and/or of what/?
      Circumstances, etc.?

"Okay, etc./Fine, etc./Go/back, etc.

 [—] prepare the ~~order~~

"ULTIMATUM AND NAMING

THE CLUMSY OBTRUSIVENESS WITH WHICH
HIS TEAMMATES INSERT A PLASTIC KNIFE ALAS
SUNJAYA, TELL ME WHAT MY SONS/<u>AND</u> THE SONS OF PANDU DID
SUNJAYA, TELL ME WHAT MY SONS AND/OR
THE SONS OF PANDU DID
LOVE WING'D MY HOPES AND/OR TAUGHT ME/HAVING BEEN
DUCT-TAPED AND/OR THROWN AGAINST THE FIRE ESCAPE, ETC.
WHILE HIS TEAMMATES INSERT MY SIN/MY SOUL/WITH
WHAT MAD PURSUIT
WITH A PLASTIC KNIFE AND/OR A CONFLICT OF/INTEREST

—transitive—

"swiss army knife/plastic knife: mixed.Media!

"Why you . . . !"

"IMPERSONATES ANOTHER PERSON/IMPERSONATES
HIMSELF/HIS OWN PART/AND/OR NOT TO INTERFERE/BY
THROWING/IT
SECRETS ON A LEVEL WITH WORDS/
THE PRINT COULD JUSTIFICATION
OUR COMMITMENT TO FREEDOM HAS NEVER BEEN STRONGER
OUR COMMITMENT TO FREEDOM HAS NEVER BEEN/EITHER AN IDEAL CASE OR
UNDER THESE CIRCUMSTANCES

"ITS SCOPE WILL TEND TO EXPAND/IN PLACE OF THE PLACE/WHICH WAS ALL
THERE COULD BE/ETC.

"IT IS ONLY RIGHT AND PROPER

"AND/OR EVEN IF HE MASTERS HIS RAGE
WHO OF HIS OWN HOLDS/BACK
KEPT TOGETHER BY/
AND/OR DOES NOT PRESERVE OUR SENSE
SHUT IN WITH GATES/AND/OR DOORS
OF THESE WHICH THE VICTIM WILL BE UN/ABLE TO DESCRIBE/
TO CARRY HIS HEARERS AWAY

SO SNUG THE JOINER/TAKING IT ON THE CHIN

"ETC."

—intransitive—

—transitive—

 [—] write down the ~~order~~

"Pencil it

            ["like, pencil it!

"Dogma alas
Oration, etc.

"If you amplify/it like this
his own flesh into/strips with a dagger alas
and/or discuss what has just
                happened/
gives them reason why they
must toil, etc., and/
or the arm which connects it to my torso
as it is and/or as it should be

—transitive—

 "HereHere

    "Was pitiful, and/or spoke to hera, his wife and/or sister

                ["his, like, wife and/or sister

"hera/juno: mixed.Media!

"Cut it! Quit it!"

    "Shucks,/recognize its permanence through, etc./
    I'll be the judge/

"A cold sweat holds me, <u>vouchsafe</u>/alas

"By reason of/
seductive <u>charm</u>/alas

"I'm
tampered with

       "Treason,/<u>vouchsafe/?/!</u>

"Else I/as alas from elsewhere
throwing out figures/remainder of/
             there being alas/nothing to remainder, etc.

"Now, "suppose," as I said, "truth is a well armed and/or dull circle:

"ULTIMATUM/WHETHER IT IS THE SAME
SHADOW
AND/OR I SWEAR/JUNO BROKE
MY SENSE/

"O CHICKEN, MY CHICKEN
WHAT SHALL BE GRAND IN THEE ALAS
MUST NEEDS BE PLUCKED AT WITH THE
CLUMSY OBSTRUSIVENESS/WITH

O CHICKEN, MY CHICKEN
WHAT SHALL BE GRAND IN THEE ALAS
MUST NEEDS BE DUCT-TAPED
AND/OR THROWN/AGAINST

BEFORE SUBMITTING TO ITS ~~ORDER~~/THAT PRINT COULD SO
POWER
ME, TO REPOSE
WHEN I SEE MY HANDS, I/

                              PICKING
A TINY ANIMAL
OUT OF ITS SHELL/

—transitive—

AND/OR THEN HELD DOWN WHILE HIS TEAMMATES INSERT
A SOUTH CAROLINA WRESTLING COACH

—transitive—

DRAGGED ACROSS THE MUDDY FIELD OF A SUBURBAN/
STATEN ISLAND TEENAGER/
TAMPERED/
WITH, ETC.

PLEASE DRINK WATER FROM OUR/
                              CUPS

—transitive—

"See?

 "HereHere

              "And/or/?

              "Your ear emits a tone you sound to hear

              "You/must be malformed somewhere

              "You give a strong feeling of deformity alas/Treason alas

"Shucks, The Macedonians obscured my vision/shielding
my eyes/human shield/?
immovable otherness of/my components alas/

                                                    mechanical

precision, etc., vision, etc./Why I'm
if I alas am uncertain/To
the best of my

aside: gravity of the threat posed by/

                                              flat

It's academic, alas
your body between/a message for you
every body's secret/weapon
and/or
drowned in a drop of water, etc.
aggress

—transitive—

asideaside: the center cannot hold/the lack of all conviction, etc.

wrong alas but necessary, but
wrong alas
aggress alas

who of his own and/or, "supPose

any impression we choose to leave/leaves an actual mark, etc.

first gives them the reason why/they must toil

before sub/mitting to its ~~order~~

seems okay, seems fine/to its own sacrifice

  [—] consider the ~~order~~

"Ostensible occasion
Oration, etc.

"So now do you doubt

" "I come across to be denied," being
and/or meaning that low/
                         blow
"Far from base earth/but not mount
                         too high

"The step is the step alas/
                    to the step

"I'll be the judge"/and/or/missed it alas

"Out of the strong encounter

—transitive—

"Ill-sounding death and/or release him?

      "Proof of no-wrong/
      "No-proof of wrong, etc.
      "Ain't/it the—

"Why you . . . !

      "Smells like/alas

"Cut it! Quit it!"

<u>Open Session GUEST PRESENTATION</u>

Summary:
Shucks, only felt as letters/strange fetters, fellers, etc.

If it is left standing, like, at all

Body:
honester honester do I saying that/I saying alas, like, alas,/what are people denying/who still deny what/people are denying/suggests inkling/suggests hint/If I point this way and/or as soon as we see this/suggests the possible/as though, like, necessary/pricking it/do you mind if I (if you) spy on you,/do you mind it?/could have fabricated/will not comply/minding it/and/or juno/broke/Where there's "smoke," there's "moke," statistically/'Twas purest light of heaven—'twas it?/Ain't it the shit?—ain't it?/

broken stones/broken blood/broken down/to components/mobile units/stockpiles/in which I discerned/cooperation/uncooperative/nothing "done," alas/each hung bell's Bow sung finds tongue/to fling out broad its name/the center cannot hold/the lack of all conviction/the lack of all conviction holds/to fling out broad/bound by/sensers/feelers/swing votes/voting/verified/ THINKING ABOUT IT/what they really believed/of their own accord, etc./signed, etc./ signed the accord: "stop THINKING ABOUT IT"/then, and/or allegedly, THINKING ABOUT IT/entertained it/tending to entertain it/knew in advance/ascertained/immune/ suggests, evidently,/surreptitiously "immune"/verified/will not, like, comply/only the letter/ the, like, rules/rules, voluntary/rules, involuntary/feels it,/so, felt it?/mind if I (if you) only felt as letters/strange fetters/these letters, statistically/allegedly/as though/taking the, like, place of /and/or to lay all flat/as though/upon no better ground/upon no ground/and/or to spy/Bow sung finds tongue/finds/everybody's, like, secret weapon/uncompliant/feels obligated/evidently, THINKING ABOUT IT/

stockpiles stockpiles/taking the place of/all other resemblances/who still deny/stipulates/as of "corn" and/or its everyday "appearance"/what is there to, like, argue?/letter of the law/commonly referred to as "knowing in advance"/that he would not, like, Help/satellite photos of/ immovable otherness, etc./tending to disobey/and/or THINKING ABOUT IT/suggests report/suggests copied/suggests almost verbatim/still true/truer/knew in advance, etc./verified/official/satellite photos/official/and/or expensive/in good stead/in any stead/findings, so far, allegedly/and/or juno broke, like/everybody's secret weapon/honester honester/like, wants to/strange fetters, the letters/fly out of/where there's "smoke,"/there's/nothing "done"/commonly referred to as "message," statistically/commonly referred to as "immovable otherness"/ so far/satellites/corn/findings/suggests/surreptitiously/conviction/upon no ground/verified/ pricking it/to fling/out broad its name/taking the place of all other mobile units/get what's coming/bound by/entertain it/sit back and/or wait/verified/what is there to, like, argue?/ Ain't it the shit?/What they really believed?/Fabricate?/uncompliant/immune/and/or as soon as we/stop THINKING ABOUT IT/voting/as though verified

There is a love that hurries me/

LOVE WINGED MY HOPES AND/OR TAUGHT ME

If it is left standing, like, at all

 [—] reconsider the ~~order~~

"Amassed
Oration, etc.

        "fetters/letters: mixed.Media alas

"To this direction/but they don't look etc.

    " "boss I'm sick"

                [" "boss I'm, like, sick"

"Stave off

"fitty cent and/or <u>Treason,</u> alas

"The swiss army knife of the absolute of Force/

"Standers by/am just the background

"It's academic

"Standers must be maintained

 "<u>HereHere</u>

"If it was and/or were to be, etc.,/at our disposal, etc.

"Whether I had/said, "Secrets,

"Who of his own will/fitty cent

"We came through/we saw amid

"So power

      "But we could also imagine a case:
      the actual/world

      "Just in case alas/alas

      "Lay/that down/prove

      "Sharp line, etc., print, etc.

"Your dove's look and/or my fox's heart

"Seems okay/seems fine
justification

:Epilogue:

[Combat-Fishing™ Homepage Welcome to the Combat fishing homepage,] [Each realized that his service was essential to combat and that he was moving the operation ahead. Part VIII: Security, Combat, Morale. Description: A report on the role of combat support units in Korea.] [Virtual Naval Hospital—Combat Stress Control] [Fighter Combat International is an expert extreme adventure aviation company] [PRIVACY AND SECURITY NOTICE. This web page is provided as a public service by Air Combat Command's Office of Safety.] [The Abu Dhabi Health & Fitness Club. The Combat Club The Abu Dhabi Combat Club. Click a song title below to download our theme songs] [You are Anonymous user. You can register for free by clicking here, The Combat Zone Online Gaming Community.] [Price Combat is search engine that compares prices on computers or computer hardwares] [COMBAT STRESS, The Ex-Services Mental Welfare Society helps ex-Service Personnel suffering from psychological injuries]

[—] rereconsider the ~~order~~

"Hi
Oration, etc.

"Barking/up alas the wrong/tree

There's no/body here but us/chickens

insofar as/sacred duty, etc., chickens, etc.

fitty cent and/or abstraction

". . . I have been donated/as I said/for example alas

["like, *donated*

"For whose fair love they
       fell

since there is no/need to alas
being what you put there

     .

                  ["what *you*, like, put there

—transitive—

"There's nobody here but/a conflict of interest
There's nobody here but/us tongues

                  ["There's, like, nobody here

"As the acknowledged/grandeur of the thing itself/
demands alas

SPEECH OF THE STONE/lyric interlude
("employs speech to represent speech")

The stone speaks:

"

Hi/
Hi/
Hi/
Hi/
Hi/
Hi/Salute [salutes]/
Greetings/Hereby/Hereby

[insert citation]

being stone and/or being made of stone/being entirely stone/stony
solid and/or hollow alas,/
        inert alas

I'm sorry/I apologize/appointed as/Regrets/to don't obey this [doesn't]

quite who is acting

trying to [tries]

know what I mean

[insert citation]

What you have seen me/"Thank you"/

backscratching/ontology/
        backscratching

        —transitive—

quid pro/encryption/inert/quid

        —intransitive—

quid/it

 "HereHere

    [insert citation]

    standards must be maintained/
    standards must be maintained/

standards must be
              maintained, alas, etc.

from being close enough [shrugs]

a dream repeats/repeats itself [shrugs]

Some form of demand?/fails
to catch/inert/quid

fails
to catch/a likeness [fails]

"boss I'm sick"/ontology

imposed on/as
                    if
from elsewhere/[salutes]

Form of, case of/
EmerGency/

know what I mean

get it [gets it]

with a spur/so/keen
Standards must/
              be
even in good/
              stead

"boss I'm sick"/say, "Thank you,"

say, "Thank you," to the nice
                    [words]

inert/

[insert citation]

"Words
are to
Thought as
Flesh is to
the Human Soul"

Thought is to flesh
as flesh is to the
human soul,
soul is to words
as to cut flesh
to cut thought

say, "Thank you," to the nice [Artillery]

say, "Thank you"
Yours Truly,
signed
signed,
          "(what
do I say)

—intransitive—

what hope my thought

aside: well armed and/or up to the
                        headlands
what my sons and/or the sons of Pandu/
a similar error to/the "same" error/torso

asideaside: became objects
as a result of/a technical alas procedure alas
missed it/
became/objects? and/or at our disposal, etc.
him/home on his shield/a thing/of
                         blood
print could/justified
, say "torso," to the nice [torso]
inert

 [—] cite the ~~order~~

viceartificer vicePresiding, artifist.
                         vicepresident

(UNDISCLOSED LOCATION)

"To all concepts/and or all sentences
Oration, etc.

" "Siege mental/wring your damn neck

" "Breast feeding/Shucks

" "YOU ACTUALLY FLY A LIGHT ATTACK FIGHT AIRCRAFT

" "SWISS ARMY KNIFE/figurehead

"diacritical mark/leave mark

"So now do you doubt
giving aid and/or comfort to
the last "Hi"

"BigTime assholes alas

                    ["like, assholes, BigTime

"Stand clear/the doors

 [—] execute the ~~order~~

"Give it!

"Give it t-t-t-o me!!

"Ahem, etc.

"Assemble presently

artificer Presiding, artifist.
                    president, etc.:

"In many cases:
could be
not-all

"In this case:
cowboy
Macedonian

"In this case:
preemptive/ablative

"Empty
                              ["like, empty]
"Suspect
                              ["like, suspect
"Pound on the table
                              ["pound on the, like, table

"May I change these garments/ablative

"New clothes, etc.,/my new clothes

"MUST   REACH   UTILITY   BELT

and/or juno *broke/*
            IN:

JUNO PRESIDING

Oration, etc.

"This training it is not/necessary

"Commonly referred to as/
"relative to"

"I come across to be"

filled in/so
            hollowed out

"Commonly referred to as/"blood from
a stone", etc.

ultimatum/whether it is the same
shadow alas
        cold sweat
while his teammates insert/
supplied with

my/torso

so power me, depending me/me power so, me depending

avail/hail/avail, etc.

benched, etc.

Supposing truth is a/current,

", what though the radiance alas
in what wild wood
traverse what pathless haunts, etc.

"as I said,"
flesh into strips/with a dagger

", what though the figures
figure it out/never/yet

"Pending alas

"Circumstances/alas/so circumstanced

"Is/anyone/here?

"Pending alas

Do Not Write On This Wall

Post No/Bills

 "HereHere

artifist.president

"Who stood the shock at Marathon
Oration etc.

"It cannot-be/that/you are wrong

"Cased:

"juno broke/Leaves no-thing un/"done"/
testifies/for/against/trivial/trivial/TRIVIAL

" "A spur so keen"/ "is anyone here"
"came to see/
                who in place"/unclog, etc.

"Reality/does not-come/the real pig, etc.
                                the squeal, etc.

"They Got/Got/

"Should be/drowned in/a drop of
                                Artillery

"The center cannot-cry/for the lack
                                    of all/conviction
"Circumstances are need to be/and/or
as soon as we see this!

 [—] execute citation of the ~~order~~

"BLAM/BLAM/BLAM/—transitive—Warning/BLAM
With this Warning/BLAM/BLAM/You are Warned/
BLAM/Beware!/BLAM/Standard practice/right of/BLAM/right/It is
only right/and/or proper/BLAM/BLAM/BLAM/
I do this for you/ BLAM/ Do
not-bother/BLAM/Do not-bother
fighting/BLAM/BLAM/BLAM/alas
Wait for/BLAM/Instructions/BLAM/Capitulate
BLAM/BLAM/BLAM/
BLAM/BLAM/BLAM/etc."

 :Prologue:
[We are here to provide global support for all combat photographers from all wars, or police actions, of all nationalities] [NATIONAL STRATEGY TO COMBAT WEAPONS OF MASS DESTRUCTION 1 National Strategy to Combat Weapons of Mass Destruction "The gravest danger our Nation faces] [Within the first few years, Busse Combat Knife Company quickly grew to become the leader in high performance bladeware. Your first choice for sword and dagger rental or sales, chain mail armor rental or sales, and stage combat choreography.] [The Internet source for the MOST ULTRAVIOLENT Wrestling promotion on the planet, Combat Zone Wrestling.] [Robots, Robotic Combat, Combat Robotics, Combat Robots, Antweight, Ants, BattleBots, bots, robot, robot wars,] [Defensive Combat Academy is no longer able to offer training to the public.] [Corporate Combat™ has been detecting and preventing business loss since 1972.] [OPCPA Awards Banquet!!! Ohio Police. Combat Pistol Association.] [FIGHTER COMBAT – AIR SUPERIORITY – BURNING CHUNKS OF MIGS] [Union Corruption: Why It Happens, How to Combat It] [Combat Shock will fuck you up]

FINAL DUET BETWEEN *ASIDE* AND/OR *ASIDEASIDE* (Redux version)

aside and/or *asideaside:*

wrong alas but necessary, but
wrong alas
aggress alas
wrong alas but un/necessary alas
Combat Shock will fuck you up
burning chunks of/why it happens/you are
anonymous user, you/can register
beat him under with hands/out of the strong encounter
fitty cents/cold sweat/<u>vouchsafe</u> the distance/from earth

                                        to heaven

the case was not-made/the case is made
Such is the privilege/Absolute of force
reckless disregard/to anyone in the/actual world
Love wing'd my hopes
and/or taught me how to
fly/as dim lights vanish in the rays of

                            the sun

FatBoy/DeathStar/rico_-chet

There always exists some specific pattern of probabilities of strategies which constitutes rational
play.   ABRAHAM KAPLAN, "Mathematics and Social Analysis"

Role playing is not a relevant factor in the formulation of a game theoretic model. It is assumed
that the players *are* the players and hence there is no question of simulated roles.
                                               MARTIN SHUBIK, *Games for Society, Business, and War*

Every Gamester will agree how necessary it is to know exactly the Play of another, in order to
countermine him.   HENRY FIELDING, *The History of Tom Jones, a Foundling*

If the activity is competitive then it may exhibit a certain instability . . . But this same instability
may result even if the activity is cooperative, provided the participants are insufficiently
informed.   HERBERT A. SIMON, *Administrative Behavior*

Even if you do not pay the municipal fee for street lighting, you might enjoy it nevertheless.
Likewise, even if you do not pay for your defense levy, you might still be defended by your coun-
try's forces . . . Street lighting and the security of the state are commonly referred to as public
goods . . . commodities and services provided by the state.
                                               EDNA ULLMAN-MARGALIT, *The Emergence of Norms*

It's too late if they become imminent.   GEORGE W. BUSH, on "Meet the Press," February 8, 2004

Love said Linger But far off the bombshells
Ardently continue to espouse their goals   GUILLAUME APOLLINAIRE, " At Nîmes"

Props: 2 people
2 cell phones
desk bell
"Voice Changer" toy megaphone, set to "Alien"

BELL/hear "bell"

Preamble [FORWARD!]: 13.3 *Is Coercion a "Zero-Sum" Concept?*

Everything needs protection./Two Guilty prisoners, against whom there is not enough incriminating evidence/possessing power to the extent that the other is deprived of it/"House wins!"/

Everything needs protection./Two Guilty prisoners, against whom there is not enough incriminating evidence, are interrogated separately/leaving it free for the other to occupy/leaving it free for the other to/give the sign,/the "language" in the "word"/Each faces two alternative ways of acting: to confess to the crime, or/to faking a thirst for itself/or to keep silent./They both know that if neither confesses, they will be convicted/[by the mainframe]/of some minor offense,/authorized by its proper place/concerning which there is enough evidence against them, and/an ice-cream cone/will be sentenced to a year in prison./The best they may hope for under the circumstances/If the motive of each is/in earshot/to increase the pay-off of the other/If both confess, each will be sentenced to five years in prison.

Everything needs protection./However, if only one confesses, he thereby turns king's evidence and is thus set free, whereas the other receives a heavy term of ten years./

Suppose first there is no way for them to discuss their situation./He himself stands to gain more/(actually lose less)/In the case of two fundamentalists/since it is clear what each holds fundamental/It might be a strategical advantage/the "language" in the "word"/what might be called man's "ideals"/so long as there are other people left over to receive

Everything needs protection./The action "confess" dominates the action "not confess."/It is not enforceable./There is no way of being sure what the other will do./This that we call/has but to open the door/the best they may hope for under the circumstances/

Let us now remove the restriction on communication:/Would this solve their dilemma?/If the motive of each is/in earshot/to increase the pay-off of the other/Would this solve their dilemma?/Who both refrain from approaching the single unoccupied seat on the bus/Would this solve it?/1 in the hand is/some of one's own pay-offs/Would this/that we call remaining intact/solve their dilemma?/out of its ruins, flames/the final front door

CONVERSATION 1 (X CALLS Y)

Y: El Paso. It's Roger.

X: Hey, Roger.

Y: What's goin' on?

X: Hey, I was wondering, ah. I have found some energy at Four Corners.

Y: Uh-huh.

X: Could I sell it to you and buy it back from you at Palo Verde?

Y: Ah, man, you know, prices are gettin' high out there. How much you goin' give me to do that?

X: Ah, let's see, I don't know. What do you need?

Y: I don't know, tell me! Hell, I might leave a hundred dollars on the table if I said something.

X: If you—if I sell it to you and buy it back from you? What are you talkin' 'bout?

Y: (laughing) Oh, man! It's what I'm talkin' about here.

X: Don't make me—

Y: OK.

X: —Don't make me look at the Oasis sites and see what transmission's going to cost me.

Y: Oh, man, don't be doin' that.

X: You're happy—I mean, 'cause we're not—we're not doin' it for, ah—we're not doin' it for congestion.

Y: You're not?

X: So, yeah, we're not getting congestion.

Y: But what are you doin'—picking it up at Four Corners and putting it into California?

X: And then what—I'm taking it into California at Palo Verde. I just couldn't get anyone to sell it to me at ah, PV.

Y: So you're tryin' to wheel it around there, huh?

X: Yeah, I'm just wheelin' it. The position we have right now it that's perfect. Um, yeah, 15 bucks! What the heck! Someone's gettin' hurt right now.

Y: Man, it's—you know, it's gotta be a mistake.

X: Ah, I don't know. It could be.

Y: It's gotta be a mistake. I mean, w—w—the next tick will tell.

X: That's true. Let's see. We can do it at—we can do it at somethin' easy, like zero and five.

Y: Yeah, but don't we have to—I don't know if that'll—I think that'll look funny.

X: Yeah, it would look funny—it—it'll make bookkeeping easy, though.

Y: OK let's—let's do like we—like we did. If it changes, I'm goin' be a mad son of a bitch.

X: If—if it changes, I'm going to have to give you a lot more money.

BELL/hear "bell"

Everything needs protection./at noon, the veiled work of midnight/*squeegee*/transcendental/WIPE IT/no doubt burning to be lifted up/It is a strategical advantage to reduce some of one's own pay-offs/zoned for double occupancy./So either way, whatever he expects B to do, A will decide to/What better side to take than/the most rational choice for each?/stay the same/ice cream cone/underneath

Everything needs protection./That there is an Altruists' Dilemma, analogous to the Prisoners' Dilemma,/leaving it free for the other to occupy./The outcome brought about when both make this choice, however, is clearly/This that we call remaining intact/clearly *les jeunes filles*/clearly worse for both than the outcome/which would be brought/about/ had they both acted *sel-fish-ly*/"House wins!"/the "language" in the "word"/"House wins!"/WIPE IT

Everything needs protection./The power of one group is always greater than zero and that of the other group is/worth 2 in the/correspondingly smaller than zero/falling through/disembowered/(*i.e.,* they hold negative power)/They'll internalize it

The leaves never topple each other, Each leaf a buttress flung for the other

Everything needs protection,/but the status/quo, albeit discriminatory, is not "bad" to one party to the extent that it is "good" to the other/worth 2 in the bush./What if everyone did that?

Everything needs protection./Either the stump yields or/the object of a threat/and I'll huff and I'll puff/is to give somebody a choice/A person P who coerces another person Q into doing/refraining from doing action A, through threatening him with sanction S/out of the mouths of babes/blowing

the whole world, light as air

Don't you hear to what soft whispers the rain has fallen/clay to clay/Everything

needs protection

CONVERSATION 2 (Y CALLS X)

X: Hey, ah, I sent the dispatch out already.

Y: OK.

X: For tomorrow.

Y: OK.

X: And so when you guys get a hold of it, um, I just wanted y—to make you aware that we're probably going to have plenty of generation.

Y: Oh.

X: So if you guys on the desk you want to do some Fat Boys or—or whatever, man, um, you know, take advantage of it.

Y: Gotcha.

X: Work it.

Y: Gotcha

X: 'Cause you guys—you're going to be there during the day, right?

Y: Yes.

X: Yeah, I don't think there's that much opportunity off peak, in fact off peak it looks like we're just a wee bit on the lean side, because they're going to be doing some work on Newman 2.

Y: OK.

X: So, ah , take a look at that dispatch sheet, and if you got any questions on it, um, give me a call.

Y: OK.

X: You can call me at 5808 or my cell number. So, if um, you know, you guys want to do some Fat Boys and start up Copper to do that—?

Y: Got it.

X: Or just wherever bi-lat market, just go ahead and work it.

Y: OK. Cool.

X: All right man?

Y: Thanks for the heads up.

BELL/hear "bell"

INTERNAL MEMO: ["THAT THE UNITED STATES UNDERSTANDS"] [PREPOSITIONS] [*PER SE*]
TO: A few Bad Apples
CC: [Line units/conducting raids]: 4 HIJACKingS
RE: *The Big Rock Candy Mountains* (5ee Appendix E: "mexxed missiges" (their sense the air/Dissolves unjointed ere))

That the United States declares that declarations of war/as their own ruin on themselves invite
That the United States declares that/and even war itself are not terms terrorists acknowledge
That the United States declares that were be1ieved t0 be needed and appr0priate at the tactical level we concur with
That the United States declares in the orthodox lexicon of war
That the United States declares 0ur pre5umpti0n 0f invu1nerabi1ity wa5 irretrievab1y 5hattered
That the United States declares that it does not consider itself bound by
That the United States understands were specifically intended to inflict severe pain
That the United States understands that power is the capacity of one unit in a system to gain its ends *over the opposition of other units*
That the United States understands could be used only on exceptionally resistant detainees
That the United States understands the authority to suspend United States treaty obligations
That the United States understands that no memorandum of understanding existed
That the United States declares External attacks resulted in causualties to the detainee population
That the United States declares that they do not wear uniforms and are otherwise indistinguishable from noncombatants
That the United States declares, "We cannot get into a situation, and I believe the family understands this, where we start bargaining
That the United States declares, "We have not been negotiating and we will not negotiate
That the United States declares, "One thing we've learned over time is that you can't negotiate with these kinds of

That the United States declares the5e are n0t c0mpeting intere5t5 but appr0priate 0bjective5 which the United 5tate5 may
   lawfu11y pur5ue

[Line units/conducting raids] [LET'S GO IN, BOYS!] [KYOTO TREATY, MOFO]

On a summer day in the month of
May a burly bum came hiking Down
a shady lane through
the sugar cane, he was looking for his _____ As he roamed along, he sang a song of the Commander-
in-Chief exercizing his wartime powers/which one participant described as "just for the fun of it"/The jails
are made of tin/and you
can walk right out again as soon as you are in/

This policy remains in Force.

On a summer day in the month of May/Sir!
Mondrian does my laundry and
A burly bum came hiking down/Sir!
in stunning London
he was looking for his/p0int 0f capture 0r tactica1 c011ecti0n p0int
as to the uniformity, its domination over the circumference,/one chemical afternoon

closely resembling or because I am having a hallucination

Stave off/does not live in that scenery
Please contact the Office of Peacekeeping and Humanitarian Operations
/"O, Jesus/Cut his mike!"

This policy remains in Force.

BELL/hear "bell"

That the United States 5pecia1 0perati0n F0rce 5tandard 0perating Pr0cedure5/

That the United States 5igned a mem0randum auth0rizing interr0gati0n technique5 bey0nd Fie1d Manua1

That thi5 p01icy remain5 in F0rce at/either in per50n 0r via vide0-te1ec0nference/effective under carefu11y c0ntr011ed
c0nditi0n5

That the United States understands that effective interrogators must deceive, seduce, incite,/as seemed, like that self-
begotten bird/and coerce in ways not normally acceptable for members of the general public

That the United States declares/which authorized interrogators to control all aspects of the interrogation to include light,
heating, food, clothing, and shelter/reviewed 35 technique5 and after exten5ive debate rec0mmended/with recommend-
ed safeguards and rationale

CONVERSATION 3 (X CALLS Y)

Y: Enron, this is Jesse.

X: We're getting whacked and exercised left and right.

Y: Oh, really?

X: Yeah.

Y: Whacked? What do you mean whacked? Can I—

X: That was earlier. We pulled that stupid Death Star. That about killed us.

Y: Yeah, on days that, ah, we think it's going to go into stage, we oughta just do a firm export or—you know, if the
money's going to be there. Or not do it at all.

X: Or not do it.

Y: Yeah.

X: I mean—

Y: I'd do a wheel. That's what we did—just do the wheel.

X: That's a bold move.

Y: I know.

X: Especially since the ISO's on a Stage 2 emergency—

Y: Oh really?

X: —state now, yes.

Y: Well, what, uh, kind of prices are you getting?

X: If we expect—

Y: —sta—any kind of stage—

X: Exactly. And I did, comin' in today, too. I should have—I should have, ah, thought about that. I knew that it was going to be hot and then after the last couple of days . . .

Y: So the Stage 1, it went into Stage 1 and non-firms got whacked, right?

X: Yeah. I thought it was Stage 2, but—you know?

Y: It was Stage 2 shortly after that. You know it did hit Stage 2, right?

X: Yeah.

Y: OK.

X: I suspected.

Y: Yeah.

X: Right. OK, who's—who's the sink?

Y: The sink is the ISO.

X: Oh, well say that's a Ricochet, at Four Corners?

Y: That work for you?

X: OK.

Y: Bye.

BELL/hear "bell"

That the United States directed the remaining m0re aggre55ive technique5

That the United States declares the use of stress positions, isolation of up to 30 days, and removal of clothing

That the United States understands interrogators are trained to stay within the bounds of acceptable conduct

That the United States declares the exi5tence 0f c0nfu5ing and inc0n5i5tent interr0gati0n technique p01icie5/interrogation techniques intended only for Guantanamo/0f varying 5everity at differing 10cati0n5/a5 a ba5e1ine f0r interr0gati0n technique5

That the United States ab5ent any 5pecific p01icy 0r guidance understands/generally because there are no safe areas behind "friendly lines"/there *are* no friendly lines/either in person or via video-teleconference

That the United Sates declares the operational order from CENTCOM/for productive interrogation/the augmented techniques

That the United States declares into question the interrogation practices of the Military Intelligence brigade regarding nakedness

That the United States understands some soldiers who committed abuse may honestly have believed their techniques

[Line units/conducting raids] [Setting: an interim site for the detainees it expected to round up as part of Operation Victory Bounty] [LET'S GO IN, BOYS!]

> Split the lark—and you'll find/parts of surfaces of material things/if Key it is, it should open/the Music—Bulb after Bulb,/you can vital these/Click "More" to see whole file/in Silver rolled

Scantily dealt to/the axe to grind/the Summer morning/*weren't nohow*
Saved for your Ear/level-set/*Dag nabbit!*/for you to think of it as one version/when Lutes be old

Loose the Flood—/potent cause of past effects/the nervous system/you shall find it patent—
harmonious repeats the shower/Gush after Gush, reserved for you—
Scarlet Experiment!/who take apart a clock to tell the time/yet there are no ears,/Sceptic Thomas!
Now, do you doubt/that your Bird was true?/which a truce/at the duty-free

BELL/hear "bell"

That the United States gaining imp0rtant and time-urgent inf0rmati0n in the pr0ce55
That the United States to increase the intelligence yield from interrogations/special information pipeline function/more aggressive methods sanctioned
That the relationship between interrogators and detainees is frequently adversarial
That the United States understands n0r were they even directed at inte11igence target5
That the United States declares current theater ability t0 expl0it detaineed5 rapid1y f0r acti0nab1e inte11igence/lagged behind battlefield needs
That the United States understands the5e abu5e5 0ccurred at the hand5 0f detenti0n 0perati0n5/in response to a data call
That the United States declares the imperative of eliciting timely and useful information can sometimes conflict with pro-scriptions against inhumane or degrading treatment/pressure was placed on the interrogators to produce "actionable" intelligence/their eagerness for intelligence may have been perceived by interrogators as pressure/must be measured against value of intelligence sought
That the United States understands the need to move from simply collecting tactical information to collecting information of operational and strategic value
That this policy remains in Force/serving as the eyes and ears in the cellblocks/adept at passive collection of intelligence within a facility/
That more information about the detainee—his mood, his communications with other detainees, his receptivity to particu-lar incentives, etc.
That the United States their purpose is to help gain intelligence that will help protect the United States

[Line units/conducting raids] [Line units/conducting raids] [LET'S GO IN, BOYS!] [HIJACKS]

Love the Drill—and you'll follow an Instinct
Blunt Edge after Blunt Edge, in credible minimum deterrence

Scantily dealt to these other continents—
Saved for your neck when released to the Press

Run me through—Who's blaming you?—
Neck in Neck, send for reinforcements—
Dry-docked!, septic Pencil!
Sad and shining *like* a wing

BELL/hear "bell"

Abnormality here resided in the psychological nature of the situation and not in those who passed through it./The most hostile guards on each shift moved spontaneously into leadership roles./They became role models whose behavior was emulated by other members of the shift./GameTown Emulation, a trip down memory lane with the Atari 2600, Colecovision, Nintendo, Super Nintendo, Sega Genesis/When everyone is responsible, no one really feels responsible./Emulation tricks the software into believing that a device is really some other device/may experience reduced self-awareness/behavior marked by the temporary suspension of customary rules and inhibitions/abusive behaviors may appear less significant and somehow justifiable/*squeegee*/when compared with/*squeegee*/death and destruction/WIPE IT/simulates the native environment in which the software runs/basically consists of finding a way to make your hardware run software that wasn't actually written for it/the confusion about using dogs/on your computer for FREE!

[Line units/conducting raids] [Super Mario Brothers] [LET'S GO IN, BOYS!]

Split the lark—/and Begin/variants of the ticking time-bomb scenario/
So come with me and we'll go and see/without any state support or affiliation
The CENTC0M War Plan pre5upp05ed that/5ab0tage 0f 0i1 pr0ducti0n facilitie5/5eri0u51y 0vercr0wded
    and under c0ntinual attack
They seek safe havens in order to develop weapons of mass/scroll down
You can paddle all around in a big canoe/you can Paddle
Keep your hands off!/
At the duty-free/you can paddle/Bodies are a strange eruption of/an extremely powerful graphics/Scarlet/
    coprocessor/Experiment!
In inequality situations/Brother Thomas/the state of inequality is not completely stable/not unusual for
    detainees to exchange their identification tags with those of other detainees
And all the cops have wooden legs/And the bulldogs all have rubber teeth/

I've practiced to feel/what looks this way/and the hens lay soft-boiled eggs
As seemed, like that self-begotten bird/a strange eruption of the State

Gush after Gush

CONVERSATION 4 (Y CALLS X)

Y: What can I—what do I need to tell you?

X: Ah, you need to tell me—

Y: —who's next to you?

X: Yup.

Y: Ah, one of them is Duke. And this is he—this is a heavy load schedule.

X: Duke. (pause) There we go. Heavy load. OK, what's the ah—

Y: So you do have a Duke?

X: I have a couple Dukes. I got—but what's you, ha—what's the path.

Y: Oh, it's um Puget generating and then it's PGET, Merrill, Avista, PS Co, Duke, Enron, WAPA. You don't have that one?

X: I don't have anything where we are next to Duke where you're generating. In this spreadsheet, he-he—this doesn't mean everything.

Y: You don't? So it might be this—this might—the one schedule I just read you first may be the one that I—

X: I don't have that.

Y: You don't. OK, do you have, um

X: Let's see if I have anything—

Y: Do you have one with Sempra that I'm ah, generating?

X: OK. Who—is Duke, ah—what—

Y: Duke's not involved in that. Sempra's next to you.

X: OK.

BELL/hear "bell"

That the United States declares that "the International Committee of the Red Cross needs to adapt itself to the new realities of conflict"

That the United States declares n0 appr0ved pr0cedure5 ca11ed f0r 0r a110wed

That the United States understands carry inherent risks for human mistreatment/under its jurisdiction or on board a ship or aircraft registered

That the United States understands/How many licks/shall be treated as if they had been committed not only in the place in which they occurred

That the United States declares that when they say, "No way, Jose," THERE IS NO JOSE

That the r0ad5ide b0mb5 and 5urface-t0-air mi551e5/have resulted in a determination that the detainees under the control of US forces were abused

That the intentional infliction or threatened infliction of severe/Convention against Torture and other Cruel

That the threat of imminent death or threat that another person will imminently be subjected to death

That to inflict severe physical or mental pain or suffering and that mental pain or suffering refers to prolonged mental harm caused by or resulting from

That the term "acquiescence" requires that the public official have awareness of such activity

That the United States declares that it does not consider itself bound by/Super Mario Brothers

That the United States scofflaw

That the United States understands the noncompliance does not *per se* constitute torture

That the United States understands for damages only for acts of torture committed in territory under the jurisdictions

That the United States understands that international law does not prohibit the death penalty

That the United States understands/or, if he is a stateless person, with the representative of the State where he usually resides

That the United States understands from applying the death penalty consistent with the Fifth, Eighth and/or Fourteenth Amendments to the Constitution of the United States

That the United States to apply to acts directed against/all members of the human family/in the offender's custody or physical control/does it take to get to the center of/

That the United States understands no exceptional circumstances whatsoever, whether a state of war or threat of war

That the United States declares that/Bodies are a strange eruption of the State/and to the extent appropriate and consistent with military necessity/THERE IS NO JOSE

BEll/hear "bell"

INTERNAl MEMo: [neither flesh nor fowl; or] [THE BUTCHER WHosE HAND] [lEIsURE sUITs]
To: detainee
CC: detainee
RE: detainee # CirCular # detainee

o that the torment should not be confined/or, if he is a stateless person/prohibit overseas sales/to inflict severe physical or mental/of equipment such as thumb cuffs, leg irons, stun belts/exhaustive cocktail/full-frontal/all-you-can

/it's so Efficient/but

the butcher whose rigid frontality I/We often hear no two human beings are alike, and thus/will sell a stun gun "kit" in which parts are shipped/tommy/separately

and yet/Am I a beggar? What is the cause? How am I crost?/all warm in the tommy barn, you face/or intimidating or coercing him or a third person/at the receiving end is immobilized for several/fires two barbed darts up to 2l feet and jolts/total exports of shock weapons and restraints approved by the United states/butcher whose/a little too subjective/merchandizing/biodegradable/it's so efficient, but/Cineplex/in 2oo2 were worth $19 million/It is often called the law of armed conflict/apparently for the sadistic pleasure of/sick for hours the butcher whose/chatroom/had recommended dogs/"NoW, YoU WIll FEEl/ the senior Army and Navy dog handlers/THE WEAKNEss oF BEING HUMAN! HA HA HA HA HA!!"/regulates the conduct of armed hostilities/acknowledged he knew a dog could not be used on a detainee/rights and obligations which/spray green foaming dye/govern the treatment of/if the detainee posed no threat/his communications with other detainees, his/*Optical, Laser-Infrared Co$_2$*/receptivity to particular incentives/laser which can heat the skin of a target to cause/tommy/pain but will not/It is difficult, however, to trace a specific device to a particular case/burn the skin/of torture. Application against the hand of a suspect/including the means for as full a rehabilitation as possible

O Australasia Less Lethal Forum/specialty impact munitions, simmunition, chemical/"Indoor use of chemical munitions"/"Opening Ceremony"/

is pleased to announce its first "Homeland Security Stocks Online Investor Conference"/because they think it will not leave permanent marks/and an accompanying PowerPoint presentation/Tactical use of dogs, advanced Taser/Click here for a partial list of/

CONVERSATION 5 (X CALLS Y)

Y: El Paso.

X: Uh hello, this is Stan with Enron.

Y: Mm hmm.

X: Hey, just wondering if I need to make the call to turn Copper on, or—or—or do you guys do that?

Y: Well, we've already given the order.

X: Oh, OK, so its uh—it's uh, getting ready.

Y: It's on its way.

X: All right, great. OK, thank you.

Y: You bet.

X: Bye.

(HANG UP) (Y CALLS X)

X: This is Stan.

Y: Stan, you think we should take Copper off?

X: Yes, I was just looking at that, uh, I think that'd be a good call.

Y: OK.

X: You want me—you want me to call the, uh, the Newman plant?

Y: Uh we can call them—

X: OK.

Y: —that's OK.

X: All right, yeah let's, uh, let's shut her down.

Y: OK.

X: All right, thanks Tate?

Y: Thank you.

X: Bye.

Y: Bye.

BELL/hear "bell"

Acoustic, Infra/sound. Very low-frequency sound which can travel/all members of the human family/the butcher whose/Airport Security, Biodefense, Biometrics, Defense, Internet Security, Integrated Security, Military, Border and Port Security/long distances and easily penetrate most buildings and vehicles. Transmission of long wavelength sound creates biophysical effects; nausea,/tommy/loss of bowels, disorientation, vomiting, potential inner organ damage or death may occur./"THEN AlloW ME To REJUVENATE YoU! ACCEPT MY PsYCHo PoWER! AND YoU WoN'T FEEl ANY WEARINEss NoR ANY PAIN!"/superior to ultrasound because it is "in band"/meaning/www.HomelandDefenseStocks.com/ that it does not lose its properties when it changes mediums such as from air to tissue./under the impression they were administering real pain to people/By 1972 an infrasound generator had been built in France which generated waves at 7 hertz./Suppose that two players with given vulnerability, specified armament, and known shooting accuracy/These individuals were told they were allowed to administer electric shocks of various strengths to some other people connected to a machine/failed to detect warning signs of potential and actual abuse/Very low-frequency sound/a one-day training session/When activated it made the people in range sick for hours

had not received an orientation on what was/the sunrise, the toothache, the lover's touch/remote-controlled stun belts/expected from his canine unit/or, if he is a stateless person

the butcher whose Def Con 1 I undergrowth/the limbo of/This is life beyond words, the sunrise, the/detainee custody and control

"To sToP IT, WE HAVE NO CHoICE BUT To UsE THE MACHINE!"

These gloves allow for the grappling of prisoners and rioters./"There is no proof our products are used/cause death through loss of coordination of heart muscle contraction/is pleased to announce its first "Homeland Security Stocks Online Investor Conference"/O that the torment/How am I crost? or whence this curse?/to the Bodies wounds and sores/for every year a fleece doth spring/Do Not Resuscitate/No connection fee/kidgloves/to torture people"

permitted American companies to ship electroshock weapons/"THE WEAK sHAll PERIsH . . . THAT Is NATURE's lAW . . ."/the butcher whose hand is sworn/bullet points/felled to make/a clearing/barcode/Cineplex opening in San Mateo/shopped it/like flies/its rump shivers, snuffling/for every year/tommy-rigged/shopped it/shopped it all around

"HoW CoUlD soMETHING DIsPosABlE lIKE YoU . . . ?"/tommy/tommy-stripped/tommy-cocked/*Electrical, Stun Belt.* A command-activated belt/*Marker, Foam Dye.* Hand-held device which is used to spray green foaming dye into the face/you are felled to make a/tommy/clearing/worn by prisoners which delivers a mild electric shock when they become combative./Def Con 1 I/*Entangler, Net, Gun.* Fires a net which entangles a human or vehicular target./relation between the angle of fire and the range of a projectile/*Hologram, Death.* Hologram used to scare a target to death./"NoW, I'll CoMPlETElY ElIMINATE YoU!"/as what he felt, did his skin/bullet points

/all-you-can-/eat/chatroom/full-frontal/all-you-can/(path-dependence)/eat

heart muscle contract-/the stripping away of clothing may have had the unintended consequence/an act must be specifical-ly intended/to include lighting and heating, as well as food, clothing, and shelter/inflict physical or mental/to acquaint thee that I intend/of dehumanizing detainees/tommy

Get in,/the butcher whose/Get rich,/hand cuts and delves into the body/adjust/adjust for inflation/Do/Do Not Resuscitate/with the black blood of black-and-white photographs/the butcher whose hand served on a tray/manmade such that they are/no humane alternative/opening in San Mateo/surround-sound/Get out

BEll/hear "bell"

> **INTERNAL [INTERNAL] MEMo:** "with the Candour of an Indifferent Person"
> **To:** dogs used for interrogations
> **CC:** *Full fathom five thy father*
> **RE:** Covenants, without the sword, are but words PowerPoint presentation
>
> can thus be seen to be self-referential, "closed-loop" type of statements/for the use of military working dogs can thus be seen to be self-referential, "closed-loop" type of statements/when everyone is responsible, no one really feels responsible/"WHY? YOU HAVE THE POWER . . . POWER THAT IS EVIL ITSELF! YET, YOU REFUSE MY COMMAND!"
>
> had recommended dogs as beneficial for detainee custody and control
>
> remote-controlled electroshock stun belts
> self-urination; self-defecation; leaves welts

THE WoRKING DoGs ARRIVED AT ABU GRAIB
IN MID-NoVEMBER 2oo3

to using muzzled and unmuzzled dogs

what trick 0f 0ptic5, thi5?

BEll/hear "bell"

Sea-nymphs hourly ring his knell/"Must be equivalent in intensity to the pain accompanying serious"/that inflict moderate or fleeting pain do not constitute/armpits, necks, faces, chests, abdomens/"TO STOP IT WE HAVE NO CHOICE BUT TO USE THE MACHINE/NOW, I'LL COMPLETELY ELIMINATE YOU!"/inside of legs/

Cineplex opening in San Mateo/with the black blood of/pearls that were his eyes/And yet am I a beggar?/Would you like some fresh-ground/tommy/with that?

/"THE NEXT TIME WE MEET, PLEASE SPAR WITH ME,/OK?"

CONVERSATION 6 (Y CALLS X)

Y: You got a lot of them?

X: What's that?

Y: You got a lot of 'em?

X: No, no, no, no, no, no, ah, just that ah, I pretty much told him what the—what was goin' on. The, ah, um, PNM was goin' from 9 down to 1, so I told him that, but I was also going to tell him that ah, ah, we were selling 50 to ah, Tucson. That should go to zero.

Y: Oh, 50 goes to zero at Tucson.

X: Yeah, that was a—that was a 50 goin' to zero.

Y: Does he know about that one?

X: No, that's what I was callin' back before to tell him about.

Y: Oh, he knows about the PNM contingent, right?

X: Yeah, yeah.

Y: So, I just tell him that Tucson goes to zero.

X: Bingo. Yeah.

Y: OK.

B: Thank you.

BEll/hear "bell"

INTERNAl MEMo: [LAST MEMO/ENDGAME]
To: Allah
CC: NO One
RE: A7; C0unter-C0unter Terr0ri5m 0p5; "Fa15e F1ag" 0p5

T0rture: dere1icti0n? 0ut 0f ta5k5? 5ign5'

5ubrepti0n, 0ut 0f ta5k5, 0ut 0f 5h0t5—Kid,

I have n0 ta5k5, 50 there are n0 5h0t5, 1ine5

0f 5ign5, fr0m y0u t0 me n0 pyramid.

F0r I have n0 b1ind5, f0r my bar5 are c0ck,

F0r he laugh5 a5 he 5t0mp5 0n hand5, & cry,

"B100d b1ue!," blue 5tamp5, hang y0u next 0r wh0 c10ck5

In next. Tw0 bar5 make H, 0ne a feather I.

Picture5 p05ed 0n hand5 & when he laugh5 a5

That cut5 thr0ugh putty, Bunny—but the pri5'ner5?—

They're cut thr0ugh, & I'm cut thr0ugh, & the bid'ne55

i5 cut thr0ugh! N0! y0u can't cr055 t0uch n0r path5

A5 want, th0 I'm n0t clear, 5tand 0n a b0x

5h0ved up a manh01e?—y0u? 50d0my & 5h0ck5.

50d0my & 5h0ck5 t0 5hit 0ut th0 50me 0ne

Fucked y0u, n0r fucked luck becau5e *they're n0t queer.*

A55ign all 5undry 5p1it
                    (1eak5—gh05t5—)—5tun

(F1e5h?), a b0ne'5, br0', a m0th'5 h01e in the gear

T5ʞ! T5ʞ!—n0 ta5k5 & t0rture'5 run? Amid

0f gun, 1ine5' cuing 5tart5. D0 ta5k5 & 5care

0ff 1ine5, each 1ine a 5ign, a pyramid

Run, run—? T0 t0rture 0ne, t0 t0rture pair?

5ay5 me! Then they—d0uble-up 5h0t5, they'll 5p0il

C0ck'5 t0rture, refu5ing it with their 5ign5—

(*G0t it*—mind1e55, t00—a5 rummy a5 0il

T0 5p0il a man dead, purp1e in the) face

0n ice t0 ri5e then circ1e jerk in 5pace

Drained t0rture—0n 5p1attered f100rb0ard5 twitch 1ine5 . . .

CONVERSATION 7 (X CALLS Y)

Y: Tommy here.

X: Great, this is Tommy.

Y: Understands that noncompliance?

X: That in order to constitute torture.

Y: Makes your hardware run software?

X: Transcendental—

Y: *WIPE IT.*

X: A theory of how a ball runs down a plane/under the impression that/they became role models—

Y: SOMEBODY SET US UP THE BOMB!

X: Place concentrated food pellets/rather than/anti-personnel bomblets.

Y: ALL YOUR BASE ARE BELONG TO US!

X: *But they never arrived at the lemonade tide,/and the jungle fires were burning.*

Y: That another person will be imminently subjected to death/incidental to/lawful sanctions.

X: They were administering real pain to people.

Y: The use of words?

X: (sung): *I paid a dollar for a ballpoint pen.*

Y: (sung): *I paid a dollar for a ballpoint pen.*

X&Y: (sung in unison): *I paid a dollar for a ballpoint pen.*

X: All righty.

Y: You betcha.

BEll/hear "bell"

> Wh0 will jerk them—1ine5!—*5hut it! What?*
> *The D00r*

> *0f the Ce11,* ga1e-f0rce t0ken, t0ken be

> What f1ipped t0 f100rb0ard5, c1ang5 0ne bar here, m0re

Bar5 there—unc0ck t0rture? Take ta5k5!—

(50d0my

& 5h0ck5, *Y0u gr0und them dr0wning,* punch t0 che5t

Catch flu? Wh0? 'gain5t a c0ck, y0u facing—W0und

5peak5: My 0pen 5eam5, 50lar plexu5, ne5t

The breath'5 end'5 a 50lar windmill 5w00ned

line5—line5—t0015 0f t0rture, wa5hed 5leep fr0m 5h0t:

F0r I had n0 ta5k5 y0u w0uld give me ta5k5,

F0r y0ur c0ck wa5 dead the c0ck cr0wed 510p—b0ught

0ff, 5t0re-b0ught 0n hand5 & cry—f0r pri5'ner5, a5k5,

Tr0t, plug plug5, a 5h0t in the arm, & h05ed?

A5 clean, t0 take h0me all th05e picture5 p05ed

"5t0mped"? Then d0uble-up 5h0t5, they'll d0wngrade part5

F0r the c0ck-fight plight t0 5tay in—
Nude—

Twitch t0 the whip, 5arge, never give in! Chart5

T0p 0ff 5ign5—F0rce flat5 5ign5, 5h0t5 prevent
—Flu

& fle5h, & fl00rb0ard5 51icked? A5 t0rture 5natched

Where were th05e pri5'ner5, br0', the t0rture caught

& the ga1e wa5 f0rced & the t0rture patched

      Up—wayward 5h0t5. N0 1ine5. T0ken? N0 5h0t—

Ye115 5arge! Then y0u—& 5t0mp5?! Tw0 bar5 make "H"

Pa5te'em in! Ma55 de5tructi0n'5 n0t a11 that

Twitche5! 5ee! They have cut5 & are buck5! T0 5tretch

0ut here, there, everywhere—Kam'ra! *c1ick5!, 10ck5!*

& the5e bar5 are c0ck & y0u're next t0 that 5cat

5trayed fr0m a manh01e—wear5 a h00d! & 5h0ck5!

A h00d! F0r y0u thi5 bid'ne55, e1ectricked buck5

"Grid10ck bump5 up c0r0nary ri5k," but

N0 51um 5um, 50n, pump5 cum t0 bum, 0r 5uck5

Wh05e c0r0nary? 50n? *50n?* Thi5 r0tgut

R0115 in the hay but the need1e'5 the t0y—

The f1u t0-day, Die, die, die, die, d0zen

Die, 5hut up, up! up! *0 A11ah,* g00d b0y

Ch005e Jew5' g1ue5, 0r 5crew5 any0ne Ch05en

F0r I have n0 b1ind5, f0r my bar5 are c0ck,

F0r he 1augh5 a5 he 5t0mp5 0n hand5, & cry

"B100d b1ue!," b1ue 5tamp5, hang y0u next 0r wh0 10ck5
     it next,

tw0 bar5 make H, 0ne a feather I.

     I have n0 ta5k5, 50 there are n0 5h0t5, 1ine5

G00d kid . . . amid . . . b0die5 in pyramid . . .

5ave'em! Then y0u, 51inging, E1ectr0de5 & h00d

It fit5 right 0ver!: hang y0u next 0r wh0 5t0ck5

Up next, b100d b1ue, b1ue 5tamp5 (f1e5h), *5under me,*

Private! Free 0f t0rture that 'p0n a c0ck,

Preened &, & brief 0n brief, & dancing buck5,

Wh0 "murder f0r virgin5"! Heaven that prime

Def10wering b0wer—Pic5 p05ed 0n their 5t0mach5

Whi1e the ice me1ted; at each b10ck a grime-

c0ated f00t b10550m5 red, Y0u 5hit, 50me 0ne

A5ked y0u, a5ked them h0w t0 fai1 t0 appear

A55ign a11 5undry 5p1it
                                        (1eak5—gh05t5—)—5tun

(F1e5h?) Ayrab5', br0', th05e m0th h01e5 in the gear

Grid10ck bump5 up, 50me 0ne'5 cut thr0ugh, pump-a

            Dicky, br0', civi1ian5 51ip, their5 i5 the

C0r0nary—50 mind1e55, t00! Heaven

I5 f0r pri5'ner5, virgin5 5ang, & 1a5t1y breathed

Virgin5 w0rking at 7-11—

Their t0ngue5, hand5, feet, b1ind5, ear5, part5 &,
            each head 5heathed

In a H00d, b1inded Inward (5ink5 5had0w

Br0ken), 5peech an ab50rpti0n 0f the m0ther-

Fucking fun 0f it. &'t 5ink5, 5ink5 be10w

0 fierce flaming pit! 5hit jammed in it, M0ther

            "501dier, thi5 i5 the dea1,
            gh05t5 aren't mi55ed."

Tw0 way5 0f b00kkeeping . . . 0ffa1 & what

G0e5 0ff the b00k5 . . . Tran5fer5 virgin5; it ma5k5,

T0rture5 virgin5 (0f c0ck—derelict—ki55ed—
     & he laugh5 a5)

5pent back5 all cracked 5ank ar0und them—run—run—

Br0ke: 5ign5, 5ign5 y0u are 5ign5, T0rture, ta5k5,
     5ign5

BEll

Prince Harry Considers Visiting Auschwitz

There are no more ideologies in the authentic sense of false consciousness, only advertisements for the world through its duplication and the provocative lie which does not seek belief but commands silence . . . The more total society becomes, the greater the reification of the mind and the more paradoxical its effort to escape reification on its own . . . Cultural criticism finds itself faced with the final stage of the dialectic of culture and barbarism. To write poetry after Auschwitz is barbaric.

THEODOR ADORNO, "Cultural Criticism and Society"

PRESENT TENSED

coming out of the movie theater the world the world is
bright too bright gnomic present tense tensile everything
happening at once the world is full of its own mute history
the fatality of reflection the fatality of nature and culture
the fatality of the German sciences of Kultur the fatality
of i.e. mute history remaining mute the fatality of of the
preposition reaching out to its object even as it e.g. it
slips away   JOAN RETALLACK, *Memnoir*

speaking so that the blank couldn't speak, speaking when one spoke [. . .] In war, we have the leisure to remember anything.

LESLIE SCALAPINO, "The Forest is in the Euphrates River"

It's a total failure of the Western imagination that the only enemy they can see is Adolf Hitler.   TARIQ ALI, *Speaking of Empire and Resistance*

Go to mass with the air
   and the shrapnel for a church
A Christian civilization
Where Pius blesses the black-shirts
LOUIS ZUKOFSKY, *"A"* 10

Vesting Order No. 126: HAMBURG-AMERIKA LINE (Aug. 1942) ThE twEnty-yEar-old princE had a surrogatE issuE a statE-mEnt indicating

quotEOnly in thE Catholic church is thErE EtErnal salvation.quotE/WhEn hE was bEtrayEd

and that it was donE in poor tastE

ThE youngEst of thrEE childrEn, JosEph RatzingEr was born/indicating that hE was sorry for wEaring thE Nazi uniform/quotEREsistancE was trulyquotE/hE nEvEr took part in any/no idEa his attirE would offEnd

ThE twEnty-yEar-old princE had a surrogatE issuE a statEmEnt indicating/his family by wEaring a Nazi uniform to a party/who won thrEE gold mEdals in EquEstrian EvEnts

quotEWhy can't wE justquotE/quotEhElpquotE him pass his art Exam/in thE khaki uniform of RommEl's Afrika Korps, complEtE with rEd swastika armband

CharlEs was also angry at William bEcausE hE was in thE storE whEn Harry, 20,/intErprEtEd thE wound as a fountain of gracE/His condEmnations arE lEgion—of womEn priEsts, marriEd priEsts, dissidEnt thEologians, and homosExuals/HE upsEt many JEws with a statEmEnt in 1987/whEn mincing around, doing that littlE flip-of-thE-wrist mini-HEil thing

ThE *Sun,* quoting a royal insidEr, said/: quotEFor it is not you that spEak, but thE spirit of your FathEr that spEakEth in youquotE

Army instructors wErE astoundEd to find PrincE Harry lackEd basic computEr skills/thanks in part to a royal scandal involving PrincE Harry wEaring Nazi rEgalia at a costumE party/WhilE it wouldn't bE accEptablE for a PrincE to bEcomE an artist/his choicE of fancy drEss costumE/wEaring Nazi garb to a fancy drEss party/alrEady has plans to sEt up scholarships for young British artists/just two wEEks bEforE world lEadErs gathErEd in Poland/to find PrincE Harry lackEd basic computEr skills

On thE samE day Harry took a languagE tEst and pickEd up his Army-issuE boots/quotEIt's not a casE of pass or fail, it's just a diagnostic tEstquotE/I, thErEforE, madE him of our TablE Round,/Not rashly but havE provEd him EvEryway

                    to pick thE vicious quitch
Of blood and custom out of him,
And makE all clEan,/
to EncouragE othErs and hElp with fundraising

hE disciplinEd thE advocatEs of quotElibEration thEologyquotE

And in thEir chairs sEt up a strongEr racE

CharlEs was also angry at William bEcausE hE was in/an anti-aircraft unit that protEctEd a BMW factory/His fathEr, also callEd JosEph, was an anti-Nazi whosE attEmpts to rEin in HitlEr's Brown Shirts/pickEd up thE offEnsivE costumE for thE party last Saturday/quotEFor it is not you that spEak, but thE spirit of your FathEr that spEakEth in youquotE/whEn mincing around, doing that littlE flip-of-thE-wrist mini-HEil thing

quotEO brothEr, had you known our CamElot,quotE/complEtE with Swastika

quotEBuilt by old kings, agE aftEr agE, so old/ThE King himsElfquotE/was influEncEd by a quotEcabalquotE of JEwish advisors

quotELast night CharlEs ordErEd both boys to privatEly visitquotE/*SchindlEr's List*quotE /quotEAlthough thE computEr tEst was a lot morE complEx than just/a quotEnativE and colonialquotE party

quotEREsistancE was truly impossiblEquotE/thE spokEswoman strEssEd/quotEthE computEr tEst was a lot morE complEx than justquotE/

quotEsEnding EmailsquotE

Vesting Order 259: HOLLAND AMERICA TRADING CORPORATION (Oct. 1942)/GeorgexW

.xBushxpaidxtribute/quotetoxrecallxthexevilxquote

GeorgexW.xBushxpaid*pays*xtributexonxSunday/~~by which investigations into the financial laundering of the Third Reich~~/toxthexsoldiersxwhoxdied*die/dying*xtoxfreexEuropexfromxNazixGermany/~~a de facto Nazi front organization in the US~~/60xyearsxagox

Thexquotebank,quotexfounded*found/made/founded*/xinx1924/wasxUnionxBankingxCorporationxinxNewxYorkxCity/axdexfacto/cemeteryxinxthexNetherlands/PrescottxBushxaxmanagingxdirector/~~for the financial architect of the Nazi war machine~~

Bushxwillxgive*gave*xhisxonlyxspeechxonxV-Exday/quoteWexcome*came/coming*xtoxthisx groundxtoxrecallxthexevilquote/Hexisxexpected*expect him to*xtoxdrawxaxparallelxbetween/Iraqxreconstructionxprimexcontractors/and/thexstrugglex againstxtotalitarianism/allxofxwhichxoperated*operations*xoutxofxthexsamexsetxofxofficesatx 39xBroadway

~~were in fact quotenominees,quote or phantom shareholders,~~xforxThyssen/Inx1928xThyssenxhadxbought*purchased*thexBarlowxPalace/quoteto xrecall*toxbe*thexevilxthesexAmericansxfoughtxagainstquote/whichxHitlerxconverted*made*intoxt hexBrownxHouse/quotewexcomextoxaffirm*negate/cancel*thexgreatxdebtxwexowe*own*them quote/,xheadquartersxofxthexNazixParty

GeorgexW.xBush/~~traveled to Berlin to set up the German branch of their banking and investment operations,~~/OPERATIONXRESOLUTEXSWORD/OPERATIONXENDUR- INGXFREEDOM/whichxwerexlargelyxbasedxonxcriticalxwarxresources/PrescottxBushxandx hisxcolleaguesxtriedxtox~~conceal their financial alliance with~~/IraqxInvestmentxandxReconstructionxTaskxForce/welcomexbusinessxpro posalsxforxpublicxorxprivatexdistributionxinxIraq/sincexthexalliedxvictoryxoverxthexNazis

Bush'sxlinksxtoxthexConsolidatedxSilesianxSteelxCompany/quoteunderscore*score/will under-*
score
xthexterriblexpricexwexpaid*paying*xforxthatxvictoryquote/Thexcompanyxmadexusexof*used*x
~~Nazi slave labour from the concentration~~
~~camps,~~/quoteAndxthexthousandsxofxwhitexmarblexcrossesxandxStarsxofxDavidxunderscore
*underscore*xthexterriblexpricequote/,xincludingxAuschwitz/~~Bush and Harriman each received~~
~~$1.5 million in~~
~~cash~~xasxcompensationxforxtheir/quotethousandsxofxwhitexmarblexcrossesxandxStarsxofxDavi
dquote/seized*seizure*xassets

quote~~Since 1939, these [steel and mining] properties have been in possession of and have been~~
~~operated by the German government~~/forxgivingxaidxandxcomfortxtoxthexenemy/~~and have~~
~~undoubtedly been of considerable assistance to that country's war effort~~quote

tox~~conceal their financial alliance with German industrialist~~/~~to try to conceal the true nature and~~
~~ownership of their various businesses~~/~~funneling laundered money and strategic materials to~~Nazi
~~Germany~~/quoteTherexwerexthosexwhoxbelieved*believe/know*xthatxdemocracyquote/~~grew rich~~
~~from Hitler's efforts to re-arm~~/~~both feeding and financing Hitler's build-up to war~~/quotewasx
tooxsoftxtoxsurvive,x*survival*especiallyxagainstxaxNazixGermanyxthatxboastedquote/Unionx
BankingxCorporation'sxhugexgoldxpurchases/quotethexmostxprofessional,xwell-equipped,x
highlyxtrainedxmilitaryxforcesxinxthexworld.xYetxthisxmilitaryxwouldxbexbroughtxdown
x*was broughtdown*byxaxcoalitionxofxarmiesquote/xwww.iraqcoalition.org/business_center.
htmlwww.fedbizopps.gov/quoteTherexis*was/isn't*xnoxpowerxlikexthexpowerxofxfreedom,
xandquote/ThexUSxgovernmentxis*will have been*xcurrentlyxunablextoxprovidexbackground
xinformationxonxIraqixcompani

es . . . forxaxlistxofxsecurityxfirms,xpleasexvisit/quotenoxsolidierxasxstrongxasxthexsoldierx whoxfights*fighted/fought*xforxthatxfreedomquotex

ThexBushxFamilyxrecentlyxapproved*approving/approval ratings*xaxflatteringxbiography/quote birthrightxofxallxmankindquote/ofxPrescottxBush/xentitled*had been titled/entitlement*xDuty,x Honour,xCountryxbyxMickeyxHerskowitz/OPERATIONXVIGILANT/subcontractor/OPER- ATIONXVIGILANT/~~long Nazi affiliation~~/thexBushxfamily'sx~~long Nazi affiliation~~/whenx therexwas*was*xalreadyxsignificantxinformationxaboutxthexNazi'sxplanxandxpolicies/*Whoxcan* could*xIxcontactxtoxfind*get*xemploymentxopportunitiesxinxIraqxreconstruction?*/evenxafterx Americaxhadxentered*had entered/re-entered*xthexwar/

ThexBushxfamilyxhavexlargelyxresponded*respond/responsive*xwithxnoxcommentxtoxanyx referencexto/businessxservicesxavailablexinxIraq/soxtheirxassetsxandxmoney/byxtwoxforerx slavesxatxAuschwitz/couldxbexwhisked*whisked*xoffshore/x

quoteWexmustxremain*stay/be*xalertquote/underxthexTradingxwithxthexEnemyxAct/axfaith- basedxstate/quoteforxwexarexconfronted*preempted*xagainxwithxenemiesxofxpeacequote/ ~~Restrictions on the right of freedom of expression, including freedom of the press/Restrictions on personal liberty/Warrants for house searches/Orders for confiscations of as well as restrictions on property/are also permissable~~/permissions*xbeyond the legal limits otherwise prescribed emergency/exception*/quoteforxwexarexconfronted*confront*xagainxwithxenemiesxofxpeacex whoxseekxtoxundermine*understand*xourxlegalxorderquote/AdolfxHitler,x*DecreexforxthexProtect ionofxthexPeoplexandxthexState*x(1933)/quoteWexcommemorate*obliterate*xaxgreatxvictoryx forxlibertyquote

ThexWhitexHousexdidxnot*didn't*xrespondxtoxphonexcallsxseekingxcomment.

ThexWhitexHouse

**VEsting OrdEr No. 248: Union Banking Corporation (Oct. 1942)a dEpic-
tion of thE sins of thE tonguE in which thE tonguE itsElf is thE
sourcE of the rEprEsEntation/**

With thE sErpEnt EmErging as a tonguE from thE mouth of Satan/quotE: I spEak my words
to thE KingquotE/ThEy may sErvE as mnEmonic dEvicEs/or vErsE 14, quotE:thEy havE
opEnEd thEir mouth against mE,quotE or vErsE 15, quotEmy tonguE adhErEs to my
jawquotE

thE sausagEs/hung from thE MaypolE/to stand for absolutE truths/

quotELikE all GErman childrEnquotE/against his will

ThE youngEr gEnEration was much morE intErEstEd in thE sausagEs that hung from/~~ArticlE
5 (1) A JEw is an individual who is dEscEndEd from~~/thosE who could climb fastEst/awaiting
thosE who could climb fastEst

thE citizEns do not act; thEy arE only callEd on to play thE rolE of thE PEoplE.

It would bE so much EasiEr for us if/thE imagE that indicatEs both an objEct as wEll as
itsElf/and consEntEd to ask for thE amElioration of thEir lot only as part of thE common lot/

ThEy had rEcEivEd spokEn or writtEn WARNINGs

PrincE Harry has flunkEd a basic computEr skills tEst/that picturEs offEr to thosE who cannot
rEad/hE touchEs his protruding tonguE in rEsponsE to thE vErsE quotEmy tonguE is thE
pEnquotE/thE gEsturE of pointing [is] an act of oral uttErancE/~~(1) JuvEnilEs, who havE bEEn
found to bE~~/whErE hE sEt up tank traps and saw JEws/~~unfit or only partially fit for sErvicE in
thE HitlEr Youth~~/quotEFor indEEd just as thosE things that arE writtEn arE nEithEr light nor
EasyquotE

holds a rod connEcting his opEn mouth to thE opEn mouth of Christ.
VErsE 11

rEads: quotEOpEn thy mouth widE, and I will fill it.quotE

thE sausagEs/thE MaypolE/thE high-flown spEEchEs of thEir
Nazi schoolmastEr

SincE no largE quantity of human bEings can havE a common will/I rElEasE thE safEty-catch
of my Browning/as an imagE of thE sErpEnt's voicE, thE tonguE/wE cannot sEE, or touch, or
hEar/Having lost thEir powEr of dElEgation,/

~~Who causE offEnsE by thEir moral bEhavior in thE HitlEr Youth or in public, and thus injurE thE HitlEr Youth~~/, sincE no largE quantity of human bEings can havE a common will/

Thinking is a form of Emasculation./**CharlEs Has InstructEd Harry**/It would bE so much
EasiEr for us if/a sign of thE purification of thE quotEflEshquote/**NOT To AttEnd Play about
Holocaust Survivors**

balancEd or objEctivE portrayal of HitlEr is nEarly impossiblE/In today's AmErica, thE por-
trayal of HitlEr and his rEgimE is grotEsquEly unbalancEd/AmErican dictionariEs routinEly
rEfEr to HitlEr as a quotENazi dictator,quotE/Action bEing bEautiful in itsElf,/whilE
dEscribing Stalin mErEly as a SoviEt quotEpolitical lEadErquotE or quotEprEmiEr.quotE/
ThE dictator EpithEt suggEsts that hE rulEd without popular support./

ThE followErs must fEEl bEsiEgEd.

quotENo namE, no namE,quotE hE shoutEd,/quotE a scourgE am I/To lash thE trEasons of
thE TablE Round.quotE/~~Who causE offEnsE by thEir moral bEhavior in thE~~/TablE Round/
quotEAnd likE a poisonous wind I pass to blast/And blazEquotE

thE Vatican's officE of doctrinal EnforcEmEnt/~~(2) WhoEvEr malEvolEntly prEvEnts or~~ ~~attEmpts~~/abortion rights/to changE thEir positions or bE dEniEd communion

It would bE so much EasiEr for us/~~to prEvEnt a juvEnilE from sErving in thE HitlEr Youth~~/to covEr Harry and William/on sEnsitivE issuEs likE samE-sEx marriagE/as thEy pack rEliEf boxEs for thE survivors of thE South Asian tsunami/~~with onE of thEsE punishmEnts~~/that picturEs offEr to thosE/criticizEd in thE prEss for hEr fashion sEnsE

thEy had rEcEivEd spokEn or writtEn WARNINGs/that picturEs offEr to thosE/WhEn askEd in a poll,/to changE thEir positions or bE dEniEd/samE-sEx/communion

, and knights/OncE thinE, whom thou has lovEd, but grossEr grown/Than hEathEn/~~(1)~~ ~~ThosE juvEnilEs arE unworthy mEmbErship in thE HitlEr Youth, and thus arE ExcludEd~~ ~~from thE community of thE HitlEr Youth~~

it rEcalls Isaiah 11:4: quotEhE shall strikE thE Earth with thE rod of his mouthquotE; or St. Paul's claim that Christians havE quotEtastEdquotE thE word of GodquotE

God's RottwEilEr/shot himsElf/adding that/quotERElativismquotE
God's RottwEilEr/shot himsElf/adding that/mEmbErship
    was madE compulsory in 1941
God's RottwEilEr/shot himsElf/hE couldn't EscapE/adding/adding
    that/To lash thE trEasons of thE TablE Round

adding that his gun was not loadEd

WhEn I hEar thE word culturE,/a bird EmErgEs from his mouth/Satan has a tonguE that is also thE word for worm in Latin/Satan has a tonguE that is also/callEd on to play thE rolE of thE PEoplE.

quotEGivE Ear, all yE inhabitants of thE worldquotE

quotEWhat I spEak I do not spEak from mE mysElfquotE

quotENazi-wisE, thE uniforms arE thE lEast of itquotE

WhEn I hEar thE word culturE,/~~who is descended from at least three grandparents who were, racially,~~/sEt an ExamplE for othErs/wE cannot sEE, or touch, or hEar/that picturEs offEr to thosE who cannot rEad/

thE LEadEr prEtEnds to bE thEir intErprEtEr./has Ears but hEars not

a bird EmErgEs from his mouth, rEprEsEnting thE tonguE of his word/

I rElEasE thE safEty catch of my Browning

quotEMy hEart hath uttErEd/I want to rEopEn Auschwitz, I want thE Blackshirts/as a sign of thE purification of thE quotEflEshquotE/litErally, I cock my Browning/as an imagE of thE sErpEnt's voicE, thE tonguE

Thinking is a form of Emasculation./It would bE so much EasiEr for us

hE touchEs his protruding tonguE in rEsponsE to thE vErsE quotEmy tonguE is thE pEnquotE/litErally, I cock my Browning

thE angEl fliEs to him and touchEs his lips with a burning coal

Vesting Order No. 261: SEAMLESS STEEL EQUIPMENT CORPORATION
(Oct. 1942)What
would
happEn to[to] thE JEws if/quotEWExmustxrEmainxalErtquotE

ThE son of[of] a rural Bavarian/public opinion poll/and his family

by[by] wEaring a Nazi uniform to[to] a party/indicating that hE was sorry for[for] wEaring thE Nazi uniform/
HE was sEnt to[to] Hungary, whErE hE sEt up[up] tank traps and saw JEws bEing hErdEd to[to]/on[on]-sitE businEss
counsEling for[for] both forEign and Iraqi businEssEs/OBJECTION

morE than half thE rEspondEnts/drEssEd as thE world's most wantEd tErrorist/for[for] thE quotEnativE and
colonialquotE thEmE party at[at] thE homE of[of] Richard MEadE/who won thrEE gold mEdals in[in]/thE
Nazi dEath camp

WhEn askEd in[in] a poll, quotEHas thE scalE of[of] thE Nazi HolocaustquotE/~~and thE ExEcution of[of] othEr~~
~~hygiEnic mEasurEs~~/quotEbEEn ExaggEratEd?quotE/a surprisingly high 25%

morE than half thE rEspondEnts/caught wEaring Nazi uniformOBJECTION/bEliEvEd/our JEwish quotE
dEmocraciEsquotEarE thE most quotENaziquotE sociEtiEs in[in] thE world/BusinEss inquiriEs should bE sEnt to[to]

In[In] today's AmErica, thE portrayal of[of] HitlEr/quotEmust havE thought HitlEr had bEEn madE popEquotE/to
forcE Catholic organizations to mErgE with[with] thE HitlEr Youth/

morE than half thE rEspondEnts bEliEvEd/our JEwish quotEdEmocraciEsquotE havE now bEcomE thE Exact mirror
imagE of[of] thE (largEly imaginary) quotENazi sociEtyOBJECTIONquotE which thEy prEtEnd to hatE so
muchOBJECTION

Mrs. Bush/thE sElf-stylEd "comEdy tErrorist" who/dEfEndEd Harry for[for] gatEcrashing a
royal party/
thE Black TiE and Boots Ball, hostEd by[by] thE TExas StatE SociEty/
.ThE raspbErry shirtdrEss madE of[of] silk taffEta combinEs WEstErn stylE with[with]/thE
world's most wantEd tErrorist
Mrs. Bush also worE a CarolinE HErrEra work to[to] thE Black TiE/
complEtE with[with] Swastika,/OBJECTIONand allowEd Mrs. Bush to appEar
slimmEr duE to[to] thE/Swastika/OBJECTIONdrEssEd up[up] as Osama Bin LadEn/
ThE color
complimEntEd hEr fEaturEs nicEly/complEtE with[with] Swastika,/OVERRULED
duE to[to] thE flowing bottom of[of] thE drEss/and that it was donE in[in] poor tastE

Mrs. Bush/What would happEn to[to] thE JEws if/if thEy can criminalizE a lovE of[of] your
own pEoplE as quotEgEnocidEquotE and quotEhatrEdquotE

If thE JEws can build thEir Hoaxoco$t monumEnts/~~and thus injurE thE HitlEr Youth~~

quotEwith[with] a fEw othErs I was happy to bE ablE to say quotE/It was thE dEpartmEnt
of[of] thE Holy Inquisition

ThErE wErE no wimps or faggotsOVERRULED

ThE Baghdad IntErnational airport is accEpting somE commErcial cargo. ThE sEaport of[of] Umm Qasr is opEn/ThE port of[of] Aqaba, Jordon/In[in] accordancE with[with] CPA OrdEr No. 38

a kindEr timE and placE, whErE/ quotEOnE night wE wErE draggEd out[out] of[of] our bEds and linEd up[up], quotE/, whErE/thEir Hoaxoco$t horror storiEs, quotEdocudramas quotE, and propaganda/, whErE/ThE picturE was snappEd by[by] a guEst/quotEstill half-aslEEp in[in] our training suits,quotE/

a kindEr timE and placE, whErE onE could throw a quotEnativE and colonialquotE party/to sEt up[up] a nEtwork of[of] Wi-Fi-controllEd, laptop-activatEd landminEs/quotEas soon as it bEcamE clEar thatquotE/

> **REutErs Photo:** NEw popE sErvEd in[in] HitlEr Youth but was not a/political risk insurancE for[for] Iraqi projEcts

> **REutErs Photo:** NEw popE sErvEd in[in]/thE Iraq campaign/but was not/influEncEd by[by] a JEwish quotEcabalquotE/in[in] thE days prEcEding GErmany's surrEndEr in[in] May 1945

a kindEr timE and placE whErE/quotEit bEcamE clEar thE photos could causE pain to[to] pEoplEquotE

What would happEn to[to] thE JEws if/thEy arE guilty of[of] thE murdEr of[of] 50 million
childrEn by[by] abortion sincE 1973/if all thE sympathy thEy havE succEEdEd in[in] drum-
ming up[up] for[for] thEmsElvEs through[through] thEir Hoaxoco$t con-artistry/should bE
judgEd by[by] thE way thEy havE livEd thEir livEs sincE/HE wrotE that rock music was
quotEthE ExprEssion of[of]quotE

you should contact thE contractors and subcontractorsOBJECTION dirEctly
for[for]/quotEJEwishquotE abortophilEs/thEy arE guilty of[of]/EmploymEnt
opportunitiEs/usually at[at] taxpayEr ExpEnsE

whEn hE worE thE/raspbErry shirtdrEss/and swastika to[to] thE ExclusivE bash/
all thE sympathyOBJECTION thEy havE succEEdEd in[in] drumming up[up] for[for]
thEmsElvEs/

What would happEn to[to] thE JEws if all thE sympathy/wErE to disappEar ovErnight
with[with] thE knowlEdgE/dEnouncing homosExuality as intrinsically Evil/that thE
Hoaxoco$t is a LIE—all LIES—and nothing but LIES?/to rEproducESUSTAINED
thE mastEr racE

Mrs. Bush/a JEw who pErformEd 3,000 abortionsOBJECTION/in[in] an anti-aircraft unit that protEctEd a BMW factory. ThE workforcE includEd slavEsSUSTAINED from[from] Dachau concEntration camp.

Mrs. Bush/whosE brothEr-in[in]-law was sEnt to[to] Dachau as a consciEntious objEctor/shot himsElf

thE raspbErry shirtdrEss/with[with] a fondnEss for[for] Mozart/narrowly Escaping thE sEntriEs postEd at[at] EvEry crossroad/spokE passionatEly of[of] nEEding to clEan up[up] thE quotEfilthquotE in[in] thE Church/swiftly apologizEd/whilE dEscribing Stalin as/thE word of[of] God/quotEpEoplE still sEE thE royal family as rEprEsEnting this countryquotE/a kindEr timE and placE

O brothEr, had you known our CamElot

Mrs. Bush/whosE brothEr-in[in]-law was sEnt to[to] Dachau as a consciEntious objEctor/shot himsElf/in[in] an ironic fashion

Mrs. Bush/whosE brothEr-in[in]-law was sEnt to[to] Dachau as a consciEntious objEctor/shot himsElf/in[in] an ironic fashion/bEcausE hE knEw hE couldn't EscapE

God's RottwEilEr/a local rEsistancE fightEr/WhEn hE was bEtrayEd and thE Nazis camE for[for] him/

bEcausE hE knEw/
hE knEw hE couldn't EscapE/

his gun was not EvEn/HE says hE

HE says hE nEvEr firEd a shot

r'pture/CENTaur

FOR THE *hibakusha*

When we claim to have been injured by language, what kind of claim do we make?...Could
language injure us if we were not, in some sense, linguistic beings, beings who require language
in order to be?   JUDITH BUTLER, "On Linguistic Vulnerability"

But the danger (here) of words in their theoretical insignificance is perhaps that they claim
to evoke the annihilation where all sinks always, without hearing the "be silent" addressed to
those who have known only partially, or from a distance the interruption of history.
                    MAURICE BLANCHOT, *The Writing of the Disaster*

1.

seeing is bereaving

eye sees only light and color and not the objects themselves   eye sees in form
more sensitive to differences in brightness   revel in the hazy light of dawn   how yellow is used to
represent light   while blue is shadow   the yellow mid-day and crimson evening   the saturated hues and the
pure whites   or should look yellow from sea-sickness   to combine the
peripheral   around an empty core or space   a sea of dots and lines   you saw it   you visualized
a map or diagram   it is the dispersion of light   you are seeing yourself move, indicated by overlap   you may look at a
bed   or slantwise at any angle   of avoiding this blindspot   in the judgment of depth   and the
faraway hills.
          Ten thousand suns   inspire the dust,   Cannot fathom, picture   alight at a point   a little too
far

2.

3.

      Isomura was a fisherman from San Pedro, CA. Kobata was a farmer from Brawley, CA. These two Issei, along with almost 150 other prisoners being a parliamentary procedure known as the "nuclear option" moved from the Fort Lincoln Internment Camp in Bismarck, dubbed the nuclear option by former Senate GOP Leader Trent Lott because it would blow up the Senate. While the other prisoners were forced to march the mile from the station to Lordsburg, the filibuster can be overridden by a three-fifths majority vote via a cloture motion. The nuclear option would allow a simple majority because Isomura and Kobata were too ill to walk. The two were driven to the front gate of the nuclear option, and that would be a ruling that the filibuster of executive nominees is unconstitutional. I'm for the nuclear option," said Lott. The filibuster of federal judges cannot stand, arriving before the rest of the prisoners. The Democrats are going to stop this or we are going to have to go nuclear. At approximately 2:30am, camp guard Private First Class Clarence A. Burleson does not have firm support among his caucus to employ the so-called "nuclear option." As several weblogs have noted, the nuclear option could come back to haunt them if they suddenly opened fire on the two men. It could come back to haunt them if they are in the minority, and if you don't do your work quickly, I will make you dig two more graves.

4.

100 Soviet MIG-15s were flying over Syria
a routine airforce escort for the President of Syria, who was returning from a visit to Moscow

a British Canberra bomber had been shot down over Syria
the Canberra bomber was forced down by mechanical problems

the Soviet fleet was moving through the Dardanelles
the Soviet fleet was engaged in scheduled routine exercises

unidentified aircraft were flying over Turkey and the Turkish air force was on alert
a flight of swans

In response to his S.O.S.
US F102-A fighters were launched; the US interceptor aircraft were armed with nuclear missiles

A normal test launch of a Titan-II ICBM took place in the afternoon of October 26, from Florida to the South Pacific
It caused temporary concern at Moorestown Radar site until its course could be plotted.

At Volk Field, Wisconsin, the alarm was wrongly wired
and the Klaxon sounded which ordered nuclear-armed F1-6A interceptors to take off

either enemy action
or the coincidental failure of all the communication systems

The effect was consistent with a power failure due to nuclear weapons explosions//a single faulty chip that was failing//the radar post had not received routine information of satellite passage//However, several NATO subordinate commanders did order alerts to DEFCON 3 or equivalent levels of readiness//but failed to reach the on-duty personnel of the early warning
During the next 6 minutes emergency preparations for retaliation

system//He was to call twice, one minute apart,
and only blow into the receiver.//saw a figure climbing
the security fence. He shot at it, and activated the
"sabotage alarm." The original intruder was a bear//
That night the aurora prevented good sextant readings and
the plane strayed over the Chukotski Peninsula//The
whole purpose of the "Hot Line" was to//of
an inadvertent war due to

during the early days of long-range radar   The rising moon was misinterpreted as a missile
                                                             attack

5.
"Please rest peacefully; for we will not repeat the evil.
"Please rest peacefully; for we will not repeat the evil.

        Please rest peacefully; for *the*
        overpressure crushes:: head dupe of heart|heart dupe of *objects*head, heed &
        do not meant by say
        what we would have you, _____ specifies
        a self-sustaining chain
        grieves
        to excess, remembers too closely, heat, hells, bells
        on your harness specifies the unconditional surrender of Japan.
        To negate something in a judgment is, at bottom, to say, "This is something which I
        Edge of the sea, concerned with itself, meant by
        meaning, In transmitting the above message, the Japanese Minister added that
        not what the sentence said but
        and so looking at this reflected image did not turn to
        with wounding self-sufficiency   stone. *Shut up!—Cut his mike!—*
        Sorry to cut you off I can't stand my own _____, go fuck yourself with your"You
        know nothing of Hiroshima"

before we knew the heart pumped blood,
it
        did so secretly

6.

When we claim to have been injured by an A-bomb, what kind of claim do we make? We ascribe an agency
     (Repaid many fold. And the end is not yet. With this bomb we have now added
An A-bomb, a power to injure, and position ourselves as the objects of its injurious trajectory. We claim that
     (An A-bomb acts, and acts against us, and the claim we make is a further instance of an A-bomb,
One which seeks a new and revolutionary increase in destruction to supplement the growing power of our armed forces.
     (To arrest the force of a prior instance. Thus, we exercise the force of an A-bomb even as we seek to
Counter the tremendous industrial and financial resources necessary for the project and they could be devoted to it
     (Without its force, caught up in a bind no act of censorship can undo. If we are formed in an A-bomb,
Then the formative power precedes and conditions any decision we might make about it, insulting us from the
     (Start; for these reasons Prime Minister Churchill and President Roosevelt agreed that it was wise to carry
On the project as it were, by its prior power. We are now prepared to obliterate more rapidly and more completely
     (Every productive enterprise the Japanese have above ground in any city. We shall destroy their docks,
Their factories, and their communications. Let there be no mistake; we shall completely destroy Japan's power
     (We do things with an A-bomb, produce effects with an A-bomb, and we do things to A-bombs, but an A-bomb
Is also the thing we do. A-bomb is a name for our doing: Let there be no mistake; we shall completely destroy Japan's
     (Power to make war. Is our vulnerability to an A-bomb a consequence of our being constituted
Within its terms? Could an A-bomb injure us
     (If we were not, in some sense, A-bomb beings,

     (Beings who require an A-bomb in order to be?

Payment Protector

Payment Protector is an account feature that can put your regular monthly payments on hold and waive interest for up to two years if you experience a qualified financial hardship

You can even activate the Plan if the member of your household with the highest income experiences a qualified event

It also allows you to take full advantage of your credit line, and continue charging while your payments are being deferred!

You have the right to cancel the Plan at any time for any reason

The bank also has the right to cancel the Plan at any time for any reason

You may find a complete explanation of eligibility requirements

You must meet the deferral qualification requirements

Loss of Job   Disability   Hospitalization   Leave of Absence   Military Reserve or Guard Call to Duty   Life Event   Accidental Death

In the event of accidental death, the Plan will cancel the balance due on the enrolled account

Payment Protector can help you through life's unexpected hardships

Why spend another day without the peace of mind you deserve

Cash or deposit the attached check to enroll

Plan for the unexpected today

reference matter

Several thousand mostly ephemeral web documents have been cited verbatim in this book.

OSI RIP(?) c.2/19/02–c.2/26/02

Results of a Nexus-Lexus™ search on content for the phrase "Office of Strategic Influence," performed on August 17th, 2002. DOD = Department of Defense; the Rendon group is a private publicity firm the Bush administration planned to hire to run the OSI.

case senSitive

A war council debates whether a case (forensic; casuistical) has been made to validate the initiation of hostilities with an unnamed enemy. This case contains inside it another case regarding whether war has already been declared.

FatBoy/DeathStar/Ricochet

The title of this piece derives from names given to games played by Enron traders in their manipulations of the California energy market. "Conversation" portions have been spliced from "the Enron tapes," recordings of telephone calls involving Enron employees that were transcribed as part of the report, The United States of America Before the Federal Energy Regulatory Commission. In performance, these conversations are staged as cell-phone calls that "interrupt" the reading.

Prince Harry Considers Visiting Auschwitz

May 8th, 2005 marked the 60th anniversary of VE Day. George W. Bush made a speech ("On this peaceful May morning") at the US military cemetery in Margraten, The Netherlands.

Each Vesting Order in this piece cites a seizure made from the Bush family by the US Office of the Alien Property Custodian during WWII, under the authority of the Trading with Enemy Act.

r'pture/CENTaur

August 6th, 2005 marked the 60th anniversary of the nuclear bombing of Hiroshima.

The *hibakusha* are survivors of the bombings of Hiroshima and Nagasaki.

Payment Protector

109

Other O Books

O Books — www.obooks.com — 5729 Clover Dr. Oakland CA 94618.
Distributed by SPD: 1341 Seventh St Berkeley CA 94710.

Towards The Primeval Lightning Field, Will Alexander, $12.00
Return of the World, Todd Baron, $10.00
A Certain Slant of Sunlight, Ted Berrigan, $12.00
Mob, Abigail Child, $12.00
CYMK, Michael Coffey, $14.00
Moira, Norma Cole, $12.00
It Then, Danielle Collobert, $10.00
Lapses, John Crouse, $10.00
Headlines, John Crouse, $12.00
The Arcades, Michael Davidson, $12.00
Candor, Alan Davies, $10.00
iduna, kari edwards, $12.00
Rome, A Mobile Home, Jerry Estrin, Roof Books and Potes & Poets with O Books, $9.00
Turn Left in Order to Go Right, Norman Fischer, $12.00
Time Rations, Benjamin Friedlander, $12.00
Startle Response, Heather Fuller, $12.00
byt, William Fuller, $12.00
The Sugar Borders, William Fuller, $12.00
DeathStar/Ricochet, Judith Goldman, $14.00
War and Peace 2, editors Judith Goldman and Leslie Scalapino, $14.00
Phantom Anthems, Robert Grenier, $12.00
What I Believe Transpiration/Transpiring Minnesota, Robert Grenier, $24.00
The Inveterate Life, Jessica Grim, $12.00
Fray, Jessica Grim, $12.00
Music or Forgetting, E. Tracy Grinnell, $12.00
Some Clear Souvenir, E. Tracy Grinnell, $12.00
Memory Play, Carla Harryman, $9.00
The Words/ after Carl Sandburg's Rootabaga Stories and Jean-Paul Sartre, Carla Harryman, $12.00
The Quietist, Fanny Howe, $9.00
Around Sea, Brenda Iijima, $12.00
VEL, P. Inman, $12.00
60 lv Bo(e)mbs, Paolo Javier, $12.00

The History of the Loma People, Paul D. Korvah, $12.00

248 mgs., a panic picnic, Susan Landers, $12.00

Curve, Andrew Levy, $12.00

Values Chauffeur You, Andrew Levy, $12.00

Dreaming Close By, Rick London, $12.00

Abjections, Rick London, $5.00

Dissuasion Crowds the Slow Worker, Lori Lubeski, $10.00

Plum Stones: Cartoons of No Heaven, Michael McClure, $13.00

The Case, Laura Moriarty, $12.00

Home on the Range (The Night Sky with Stars in My Mouth), Tenney Nathanson, $12.00

Criteria, Sianne Ngai, $11.00

Close to me & Closer . . . (The Language of Heaven) and Désamère, Alice Notley, $12.00

Catenary Odes, Ted Pearson, $12.00

Collision Center, Randall Potts, $12.00

Light, Jerry Ratch, $12.00

(where late the sweet) BIRDS SANG, Stephen Ratcliffe, $12.00

Tottering State, Tom Raworth, $15.00

Kismet, Pat Reed, $12.00

Cold Heaven, Camille Roy, $12.00

The Seven Voices, Lisa Samuels, $12.00

Crowd and not evening or light, Leslie Scalapino, $12.00

Enough, an anthology edited by Leslie Scalapino and Rick London, $16.00

O ONE/AN ANTHOLOGY ed. Leslie Scalapino, $12.00

O TWO/AN ANTHOLOGY: What is the inside, what is outside?, ed. Leslie Scalapino, $12.00

O/4: Subliminal Time, ed. Leslie Scalapino, $12.00

War and Peace, ed. Leslie Scalapino, $14.00

The India Book: Essays and Translations, Andrew Schelling, $12.00

" . . . But I Couldn't Speak . . . ", Jono Schneider, $12.00

Rumors of Buildings To Live In, Keith Shein, $12.00

A's Dream, Aaron Shurin, $12.00

In Memory of My Theories, Rod Smith, $12.00

Partisans, Rodrigo Toscano, $12.00

Lilyfoil, Elizabeth Treadwell, $12.00

trespasses, Padcha Tuntha-Obas, $12.00

Homing Devices, Liz Waldner, $12.00

Picture of The Picture of The Image in The Glass, Craig Watson, $12.00